The Other Side of the Aisle

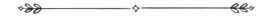

Reflections on life, love, and the business of brides

Tobey Dodge, CSEP

authorHOUSE®

AuthorHouse™
1663 Liberty Drive
Bloomington, IN 47403
www.authorhouse.com
Phone: 1 (800) 839-8640

Published by AuthorHouse   01/06/2016

Library of Congress Control Number: 2015913327

ISBN: 978-1-5049-2137-4 (sc)
ISBN: 978-1-5049-2138-1 (e)

Edited by Marianne Cotter
Cover Concept designed by Tanya Bryan

Print information available on the last page.

Even though the stories recalled in The Other Side of the Aisle are based on
multiple actual weddings with similar themes, many of the settings, circumstances,
occupations, and other concrete details have been altered in an attempt to create a
level of universality for the reader while exercising literary license for privacy.

Contents

Dedication

This book is dedicated to:

Pat Conaway, my first mentor and business confidant

Cary Gursey, of Happy Times Video Company who instilled greater confidence in my abilities by giving me an opportunity to work on high level weddings.

Jeff Ames, who inspired me to begin writing, selected the title of this book, and was my closest friend and colleague for 15 years.

To my colleagues who have worked side by side me for so many years. Your dedication to excellence gave me great support and comfort knowing that you were always there for my clients, and gave me so many opportunities to work with you.

To my Clients who invited me to assist them at one of the most important moments in their lives.

And finally, to my family that spirited me on and on never doubting I would finally finish this book.

Preface

Some ten years ago my good friend and long-time colleague Jeff Ames and I set out to write a book together about the wedding industry. If you knew us when we started, you would have said we were a classic "odd couple." Jeff was tall, with an aggressive nature at times, and fastidious to the point of annoyance. His business model was minimalist: He a top flight DJ and veteran entertainment specialist for nearly 20 years, kept paperwork, meetings, and communications with his clients simple and direct. I a seasoned wedding planner of the same vintage, joined every professional group in the industry, and was famous for penning endless email threads, most posted from an office that resembled a corn maze with circuitous paths leading to my desk and then to a closet that was stacked high with client files, magazines, and linen sample books.

While I had an active presence on most social platforms, Jeff operated without a website until his friends shamed him into getting one. He loathed even email. For Jeff social engagement was old school: talking on the phone and lunching with industry friends to keep up relationships and stay current on gossip and goings-on. With nerves of steel and a biting sense of humor, he saw life in only two shades: black and white. God forbid you tried to serve him fish (my personal favorite) rather than a man-sized burger, medium rare with fries, please.

Despite the fact that we were both tall, we made an unlikely pair - picture Don Draper from "Mad Men" teaming up with the Good Witch Glenda from "The Wizard of Oz" to do anything together. But somehow we just clicked as friends and colleagues. We would talk most Monday mornings to critique the weddings we worked on together or swap stories about the events we worked on separately relying on each other for insight and empathy.

He could say just about anything to me and I could do the same to him without fear of reprisal. There were times when we saw things differently and acted more like squabbling siblings than wedding pros, but underneath it all we respected each other immensely and drew strength from each other. So we set out to give something back to the industry we loved by writing a book explaining how the industry works from the inside out, in essence why things are the way they are when it comes to planning a wedding and working with wedding sites and services.

After writing several chapters, we sent our precious words out to two editors for feedback: Was our concept viable? Would our book find an audience? Now mind you, this was before the era of reality TV: No wedding reality shows or real-wives-of-whatever-city-comes-to-mind dramas.

The comments that came back were as different as Jeff and I in personality and point of view. One editor didn't think my voice came through strongly enough in the writing. The other editor thought Jeff's writing was too negative and would not be well received. We both recognized that there was truth in what was shared with us, but we weren't sure how we were going to bridge the gaps.

We took the next year to think about how to structure a book about "He said she said, instead of intertwining and agreeing on everything in the book.

As so often happens in life, fate intervened.

About a year later, Jeff was working at a wedding in downtown Los Angeles when he began having chest pains. He started sweating profusely and felt weak. His trusted sidekick/assistant was there and could have taken over the job that night, but Jeff just sat down for a while and got through the gig. When he finally saw a doctor, he got confirmation of what all of us close to him had surmised; he had had a slight heart attack. What came next, no one could have predicted.

As the doctors reviewed his x-rays and blood tests they found something unexpected: Jeff had lung cancer. Due to the placement, size, and type of cancer cells, operating and even radiation was ill advised. Chemotherapy was his only chance. After downing several chemical cocktails, to no avail, he went to Germany to undergo experimental treatments. All efforts proved to be futile. It was now Jeff's job to make God laugh and share the weekend's adventures on Monday mornings.

Even though the book you are about to read is a departure from our original concept, I believe Jeff is looking down on me thinking, " 'at a girl, finally Tobey found her voice!"

Section 1

Looking Back, Living Through, Going Forward

Chapter 1

A New Direction in Writing

In the beginning of our journey together, my editor Marianne observed, "Tobey, there isn't much of you in this book. You described events colorfully and the writing has a nice energy, but there's scant little of you interjected into the stories. After all, it is a memoir, right?"

I took a hard swallow listening to Marianne. I knew I wasn't a natural writer, but at times I felt Marianne's edits reflected her attitude instead of mine. Frankly, as my editor she had to put her mark on the writing since I had abdicated that role. What she was really asking was how *I felt* about the situations I was sharing in the book.

After much introspection, I realized that she was stone cold correct in her assessment! I had been behaving like a neutral correspondent reporting about couples and their weddings. Oh sure, I wrote about funny situations that teetered on the brink of disaster, but in my initial chapter drafts I hadn't shared my own gut reactions to any of the circumstances I experienced during 27 years working with brides, grooms, and their families.

The last thing I wanted to do was to betray a former client's trust by exploiting their foibles of their wedding day. Oh sure, I had my Monday round ups with trusted friends and colleagues dissecting the triumphs and near tragedies that were narrowly averted, but to tell the public at large how I felt was a line I wasn't sure I wanted to cross. Someway I had to find a way to express my feelings and talk about the issues that would be helpful to future brides and grooms and their families without divulging personal information for sensational impact.

For all my friendliness and outward appearance of confidence, I strive to avoid stress and criticism. I like being where the action is - in the mix so to speak - but to hurt or disappoint others is the worst outcome for me – personally and professionally. I have strived to find a balance in this book by sharing many typical situations I came across working with nearly 800 couples.

As a natural problem solver, I'm always ready to give an opinion whether asked or not. Fortunately, over the years I've honed my instincts as to when to open my mouth and when to keep it shut. (More about that later in the book.) I would rather provide insights than negative criticisms. For as strong as I sometimes have to be on the job, I have little tolerance for friction or conflict.

Can you blame me? I grew up the middle child of three sisters. I was sandwiched between two exotic brunettes, each one intelligent, gifted, and gorgeous. My best chance of getting a word in edgewise and receiving occasional praise came from my ability to make friends and be diplomatic; classic characteristics of my middle-child ranking, or so I've been told.

In school, I was used to working hard for "B's" and in some cases even "C's," especially in math and foreign languages, but I displayed having artistic tendencies and loved working with children. I made it through college, got a teaching credential, and embarked on a career as a middle school art teacher.

I probably would have remained an art teacher forever if life hadn't insisted on happening. An hour and a half commute to my teaching position proved to be too challenging while also working on repairing a fixer upper home and trying to be the perfect wife and daughter-in-law.

I had intended to return to teaching once our children were of school age, but then my husband needed help in his family's business, giving me the chance to design kitchen and gifts items. After nearly 16 years of marriage, as I nudged the 40-year mark, my husband found a better love match with his office manager. It was a big shock at first.

All the effort, love and devotion to making things work just didn't help make it work after all. My confidence and self-esteem were in the basement.

I had to face the daunting task of marketing myself in the real world after having worked under the radar without a paycheck for nearly 10 years. When my husband left, my kids were 5 and nearly 10 years old, attending two different schools. I thought I could fall back on my teaching skills. No such luck. In the mid-eighties, much like now, teaching jobs were scarce, especially in the arts. Divorced with two children after nearly 16 years of marriage left me with a lot of gaps in a formal resume.

I had enough gumption to speak with the administrators at a few local schools. They all treated me well, and I was frankly gratified by their receptivity to my real-world experience doing product design. I had traveled to Asia and Europe to work with manufacturers to bring products to market. No one ever asked me what I earned, sparing me the humiliation of admitting I was an unpaid spouse.

The bottom line was simple: No permanent art teaching jobs were available in my area. Even had I been fortunate enough to be hired, layoffs were looming and the "last hired, first fired" policy was sure to knock me out of any new teaching position I could manage to land. One junior high principal said something I will always remember. "Tobey, as much as I would like to hire you, if you can find a way to do anything else, then do it." I didn't know how important those words were then, but I did hear them and that remark has stayed with me ever since. Without the job, your dream job is no dream at all.

I began a quest to find a job that would suit my reluctant new status in life. My aunt Ethel, who lived nearby, came up with a suggestion. She knew of a print shop that had a graphic arts department on the second floor. The manager wanted to bring someone in to act as a liaison between the printing and design departments as well as sell graphic sales.

Because I had specialized in classical printmaking in my last two years of art college, the idea of working in the printing business held a special appeal for me. I visited the shop and met with the owner,

Margret Weinstein. After a three-hour interview, she hired me as a utility player selling graphic services and acting as the interdepartmental fixer of miscommunications. I was also quickly appointed the shop OSHA rep. I realized, however, that the sales part of the job came with a big learning curve.

Having literally been the boss's wife for many years, I had never faced much acrimony or personality challenges in the office so I was dismayed to encounter the deep underlying mistrust between departments in my new job. Worse yet were the verbal battles frequently pitched between departments over minor differences before the facts were sorted out. The bickering and intolerance I observed reminded me of my own flawed marriage. I had to face the fact that I had been, in essence, fired as a wife. I didn't want to be fired ever again for any reason. I had to get a handle on the working relationships in the office or look for another job.

My strategy was to become a better listener and it paid off. The lunchroom conversations verified my suspicions that others were struggling with varying degrees of domestic stress. I figured if I could foster an environment of understanding among the staff, they would begin to trust each other enough and begin working as a real team.

However, the problem went right to the top. When irritated, the owner could be short tempered with quick mood swings and a sharp tongue. Even though I accomplished what I was asked to do, Margaret reprimanded me for being too social in my efforts and barred me from entering the design shop area. To communicate with my immediate superior or the other designers I had to call the design department over the phone. So much for the personal touch. It was a humiliating experience.

At first I felt I was being punished for doing the very thing I was hired to do. I took the comments and criticism to heart in order to change my behavior. I felt I had no choice but to take a good long look at myself and determine if I could survive, much less thrive, in this environment. If not, it was time to forge another career path.

Over time, the owner softened a bit and I was able to venture back into the graphic design department to speak directly to the designers. Still, after two and a half years in the printing business, I recognized that advancement was not possible for me. Then I got wind of an impending sale of the business and began to prepare for another change.

I looked into home-based businesses, thinking I could build a venture on the side until it was established enough for me to quit the printing job and become fully self-employed. I had abandoned the dream of going back to work as a teacher because I was unwilling to move out of the area or even to another state. I tried selling survival packaged food sales, in-home water filtration systems, leasing fine art to corporations, and selling travel club memberships, but nothing clicked.

It was time for some serious soul searching. I sat down with pen and paper and on one side of the page I listed all the things I was good at, enjoyed, and was willing to do to make money. On the other side, I wrote out all the skills I needed but didn't possess. How could I acquire those missing skills? Could I find a way to make enough money to keep the kids and myself afloat?

I decided to take a six-week career guidance course in the evenings to figure out what aptitudes I might have overlooked and to boost my confidence. Perhaps I would discover a hidden talent. I exposed myself to a battery of tests which revealed that I had missed my calling as an architect. Apparently I have an uncanny knack for spatial relationships, but I would have to sharpen my math skills if I wanted to get serious about becoming an architect.

Soon it was clear that I possessed neither a burning desire to become an architect, nor the patience and funds to pursue such a lofty endeavor. In the end all my efforts to redirect my career came down to a twist of fate. My future career walked into the print shop in the form of Reverend Bard Green, a kindly man who connected me to an opportunity of a lifetime.

The print shop had occasional walk-in customers who needed business cards. Reverend Green came into my glass cubical and in a soft voice apologized for not having an appointment. Then he explained that he just needed to update the address on his cards. In the process of helping him I learned that during the week he sold promotional items to businesses but on the weekends he officiated wedding ceremonies as a non-denominational minister.

When he returned a few days later to pick up his business cards he gave me a bit of a jolt when he said I had the perfect personality for weddings. Little did he know what I had gone through in my marriage, but just the same, I thanked him for his kind remarks. He said he knew a woman who was new to the wedding industry and needed some help. Reverend Green said he would like me to meet this lady at the local Chamber of Commerce luncheon the following week.

Since I often sat in for the printing shop owner at such meetings, I said sure, but I knew full well I would need to tell the owner of the wedding business that I didn't have any professional experience in the wedding industry.

Reverend Green wasted no time in introducing me to Millie Annenberg at the start of the luncheon. She had a quick smile and an infectious laugh. She wanted to know what I knew about weddings. I told her I had helped several friends with their weddings and had volunteered at our community center for special events, but I didn't have broad knowledge about traditions or other cultures. Within ten minutes, Millie had asked me if I wanted to work for her. I was stunned. I asked her if I could visit her store, Wedding Dreams, and learn a bit more of how I could be of service to her.

Her shop was nestled in among several other wedding-related businesses in a grouping of two-story buildings designed in a style reminiscent of the French Quarter in New Orleans. The entire store was only about 300 square feet, but the walls were lined with mahogany bookshelves full of photo albums from photographers and florists. The store was set up as a resource library where brides and grooms could come in, look at photography, flowers, invitations books and portfolios etc. and learn about their choices in wedding locations and services. These wedding vendors paid Millie a monthly advertising fee to display their business information. She also facilitated meetings between wedding service providers and potential clients by providing space for them to learn about each other and possibly contract for services.

Millie wasn't able to offer me a full-time position, but I really liked her and I asked if there was anything else I could do for her. To my surprise she said yes. She needed someone she could recommend to help the brides and grooms get down the aisle. I asked her what I would need to know to do that professionally. She threw a couple of books and video tapes into my arms and said, "Look at these. If the work interests you, give me a call and we will work something out."

After reading the books and viewing a couple of videos, I thought it looked like fun and I told Millie I wanted to give it a try. She introduced me to managers of a large family-owned banquet center and a nearby synagogue. I was accepted at both places and for two years I gave Millie a 20 percent commission for each event I was hired for at these two sites. Once I got my footing and was consistently booking wedding day coordination at other sites, I went to a monthly service fee.

I would never have knocked on the doors that Millie opened for me on my own. I will always be grateful to Reverend Bard Green and Millie Annenberg for seeing something in me that would lead to a wonderful career as a wedding planner that would last for more than 25 years.

It took me four years working three jobs to finally take the plunge and devote myself to my wedding business. The path was littered with ups and downs and tough decisions. How would I finance this business? Is this the best I can do for my kids? Would I be asking my kids to sacrifice not only quality time with their mom but material goods, as well, as the business moved toward profitability?

Since weddings were booked so far in advance I had to accept that I would likely miss out on family events that were bound to pop up on the same day or weekend of a wedding. In essence I had to ask myself what it would take for me to build this business into a sustainable source of income and a meaningful and fulfilling career.

When I look back, I wonder how I was ever able to do it: Build a business, raise two children, and find love and marriage along the way. I know one thing for sure. Without the help of those who gave me my start and the support and friendship of a wonderful core group of friends I worked with in the wedding industry, I wouldn't have been able to accomplish what I did.

Hopefully this book will be an instructive memoir for those who may gain insight from my personal perspective about the world of weddings. I am, at this point, a seasoned wedding planner. I want to share many lessons I learned along the way with my perceptions as to how individual personalities, attitudes, and values shape the wedding experience for client and planner alike.

Chapter 2

My Parents' Entrepreneurial Blueprint

Over the years, my parents, Alice and Bernie, were active in many religious and civic organizations. I saw them organize many events and parties for our family, friends, and community. My early childhood was filled with the excitement of these festivities inside our home and at banquet centers and clubs. In essence, my parents were known as doers.

I followed in my parents' footsteps when I was a part of creating one of the first tutorial projects as a junior in high school in 1965. I took President Kennedy's words very seriously that as Americans we had a duty to do something for our country. I enjoyed being around children and I knew I wanted to be an art teacher, so I thought perhaps I could organize a program to help kids after school in nearby grammar schools. I got the support of my high school administration and went to work developing the program that was the forerunner for future programs across the city. I even got school elective credits for doing so. Being able to work on the project during school hours left time for my other activities that included a part-time job at a nearby pharmacy in the evenings and on the weekends, membership in a YWCA youth group, and school politics. With so many activities, I know my grades suffered from time to time, but I always wanted to live a full and purposeful life. I didn't want to miss out on anything.

A decade earlier I had been confined to a hospital bed as a polio patient. Shortly after I fell ill, researchers began testing the Salk vaccine that would eventually eradicate the threat of polio in the U.S., but I would not benefit from that. I remembered missing my family and friends and wondering if I would ever rejoin the neighborhood kids in backyard games. Some of the children I met in the hospital were never able to ride bikes as I did.

I was one of the lucky ones. I left the hospital with no visible after effects to continue rehab at home, having missed only a good part of one semester of the first grade. Once I came home, not wanting to fall behind in school, I asked my mom to read to me from the books my classmates had heard the teacher reading to them. I listened to her say each word, trying to memorize each passage. We reread the books every day until I was allowed to go back to school.

After several readings, I began to learn the words and could read them out loud with some confidence. My biggest fear was being asked to read aloud in front of the class. I had missed the lessons on the basics of phonics and didn't know how to sound out unfamiliar words.

Rather than seeking help from my parents or teachers, I kept my fears to myself. I didn't realize it at the time, but polio wasn't my only problem. I later learned that I had a learning disability that affected my comprehension and how I processed information. I just thought I was a slow reader or slow learner.

I compensated by studying longer and harder to get good grades. Like most kids, I didn't want to be different. Being very tall for my age with tight frizzy hair, buck teeth, and a husky build made me a conspicuous target for bullies. I didn't want to be held back a grade and stick out even more from my classmates.

I had learned through my parents how important it was to not envy others. As the family mantra ran, there will always be someone who has more or less than you have, so be happy with what you have. If you want something more, work for it. The postscript was that when we were doing well, we had a duty to give back to our community.

I also recognized that when my parents were doing well in business, we enjoyed extras such as housekeepers, big backyards, and new bikes as soon as we outgrew the smaller ones. Good times also brought more people to the dinner table. Close friends were more like family. Mixing business with pleasure became a way of life. I often played with the children of my parents' business associates, and we attended each other's birthday parties. Stacks of 16- and 8-millimeter film reels, archived and shelved for posterity, commemorate these celebrations with kids skipping to "Ring Around the Rosie," swinging bats at piñatas, and blowing out birthday candles.

When times got tough, the circle of friends got smaller and we had to become more self-reliant. We kids collected pop bottles to earn spending money. When our mother joined the workforce to supplement our father's income, we became latchkey kids, letting ourselves into the back door after school. I learned to sew my own clothes and hand-made presents were encouraged. We tried to draw strength from each other. Scrambled eggs and hot dogs were staples for dinner from time to time. Elaborate outdoor birthday parties were replaced with single-layer cakes shared at the dinner table and fitted with two extra candles, one for good luck, and another to grow on.

To my surprise, my adult life today mirrors my parents' lives in more ways than I could have imagined. Most of my closest friendships consist of the business associates I work with day in and day out over the phone, through emails, and on event days. The monthly networking meeting and non-profit organizations I participate in aren't all that different from the community work my folks supported many years ago. They received acknowledgement for their good deeds, as I have, but more importantly they realized that nothing is forever and you have to take responsibility for your choices and be open to change, even if it's not comfortable or easy.

I learned these lessons by observing how my parents worked through family challenges and how they dealt with the inventible economic cycles that can reduce the prosperous to paupers if they don't adapt; Likewise, the emotional seismic shifts that shake up our private lives for better or worse.

My father was a natural entrepreneur and, some would say, a Renaissance man. He inherited a creative, artistic bent from his own father who got his start in America from Germany painting murals and frescos on church ceilings. My grandfather sang in the New York City Opera Chorus and was known to throw wonderful parties and celebrate holidays with great panache.

My dad tried to follow in his footsteps but was told his voice was unsuitable for further development. He turned to his other talents; he loved to paint and draw and was a natural athlete. He was a superior speed skater but had to give that dream up when the family fell on hard times during the Great Depression.

As the specter of WWII edged out the Depression, he set aside another dream, that of becoming a chemist, instead managing the soft goods department at a major department store in New York City while working a defense job at night, all while continuing to help his dad out in his business. It wasn't unusual for most young men who grew up in the '20s and '30s to have more than one job to make ends meet. They knew that life could change on a dime and they had to be prepared for the worst while making the most of the best when it came around.

My mother moved to Pittsburg when she graduated high school to get a job and lived with her aunt and uncle. It was at their house on New Year's Day in 1940 that she met my father, the son of a business associate of her uncle's who had invited my father's father over for a business lunch.

She was a mature eighteen years of age, having lost her father to a heart condition that was exacerbated by a mustard gas attack he endured while serving in Europe in the First World War. She was just nine when he died and she helped raise her younger brother while her mother worked in a market to keep the family afloat.

Having heard that this young lady had won a beauty contest, my future dad was intrigued and wanted to meet her. He jumped at the chance to tag along with his dad to meet her. Little did my mother and father know that her uncle and his father set up this lunch so they could meet.

Well, it was love at first sight. My dad, thin from working three jobs, was never the less handsome with his wavy black hair, deep brown eyes, and a thin mustache reminiscent of the dashing David Niven (for those who remember). As for my mom, she resembled Norma Shearer with a wide yet delicate smile and a light that danced in her eyes.

They saw each other just four times before they were married in May of 1940. My mom's sole ambition was to be a housewife and mother. With the U.S. entering World War II, my dad decided to enlist in the Navy instead of taking his chances on being drafted into the infantry where he might find his flatfeet in the muddy trenches.

As it turned out, my dad didn't have to serve in the Armed Forces at all. The day before he was to report for boot camp, he listened in shock to a radio announcement declaring that men who were over 25, had a defense job, and a child born before Pearl Harbor, were exempt from military service. The news left my parents elated and overwhelmed. My dad had already left his day job plus they had given up their hard-to-find apartment. And still he felt a strong obligation to sustain the entire extended family. The defense job wasn't enough income to help out his parents, so he continued his defense job and went full time in his father's business.

By the end of the war, our family took a turn west to California. My father figured that the weather would be better for his ailing father and hoped there would be opportunities for everyone. Once in California he helped his father build a paint contracting business that was successful enough to take care of two families.

Within the first decade back in California, his father passed away and now had the responsibility of two families on his shoulders plus one of his sisters, and a step-father-in-law of my mom. Our family was literally busting out of the seams. Out of necessity, my mom's desire to be a stay-at-home wife had to change. My dad opened a toy store called Alice in Wonderland and needed my mother's help.

At heart, my father was an inventor, a passion that allowed him to bring his other abilities together. In the toy store he spent several years observing how children played with toys. He was always looking for ways to improve product design, and not only with toys. The chemist inside of him emerged as he experimented with creating different textures with paint, making it look like marble and other materials.

Reluctantly, my mom ran the day-to-day business of the toy store while he looked after the paint contracting business.

The winds of change visited our family again when my parents had to relocate the toy business because the space they rented was being demolished. They moved the business to a smaller space in a higher rent area, but found that the toy market in the new neighborhood was completely different. In the original location the local kids wanted bicycles, toy guns, and dolls. In the new area parents favored educational toys, board games, and creative art activities.

Suddenly their business was in peril. My parents dug themselves into a financial hole they couldn't get out of. When my father had to declare bankruptcy my mother suffered a nervous breakdown and didn't leave the house for one year. Our family doctor wanted to send her to a sanitarium, but my dad refused and we all pitched in to help her through that time. Even then I was aware that my mom was mourning the loss of her youth, her lifestyle, and her friendships. She went for a whole year without getting a haircut too.

Today I believe her depression went much deeper. She felt she had contributed to the failure of the business, not its success, and the stigma of bankruptcy left her feeling alienated, helpless, and ashamed. She had never quite recovered from the early loss of her father and when she was 26 she lost her mother.

My father, being more resilient, was convinced he could make a new start by presenting his toy inventions to manufactures. He was trying hard to make one of his dreams come true.

Once he was back on his feet, this time as an independent paint contractor, it was time to make one of those inventions profitable. In the summer of 1960 when I was twelve and my younger sister, Barbara, was eleven our parents took us along on a creative business road trip. My older sister, Merill, had decided to move out on her own upon graduating from high school. She managed to obtain a high-level security clearance working for Systems Development Corporation in their library of documents at the tender of 18 while starting college at night. Now that takes guts! She was a trailblazer back then and quite a tough act to follow as I grew up.

Our two-month trip turned out to be the experience of a lifetime, especially for a young person. It was my job to write a journal about our adventures and to keep a log of our expenses. From Winnemucca, Nevada to New York City and back, I learned so much about American history and how people in different places lived by experiencing regional foods and taking in the sites with my mom and sister while my dad went from one interview to another, introducing his ideas for futuristic toys.

Unfortunately, the business didn't pan out in reality as it had promised on the drawing board. My dad lived out the last 20 years of his business life as a paint salesman and later as the west coast sales manager for an East Coast paint company. But the lessons I learned from his experience stayed with me a lifetime. I saw first hand what it's like to go after a dream, do your best to get it off the ground, and then to fail — only to try something else and survive.

I remember my mom telling me throughout my childhood to be more like my dad. She didn't want me to be saddled with the insecurities she had about herself. A painfully shy person, she never wanted to work with the public. After the failed toy store and manufacturing episodes, my dad never asked her to help him in business again.

Once my younger sister, Barbara, and I were in junior high school with college on the horizon, my mother's determination to see all her daughters go to college fueled her decision to overcome her fears and get a job in a local department store to help pay for tuition and books. She started by selling blouses. While she didn't like working with the public, she was a closet clothes junky. The job provided her with discounts on clothing that allowed her to indulge her love affair with shoes and purses.

She would take us clothes shopping as soon as the new fall merchandise came in July, using her Christmas Club money or lay-away plans to pay for a few new outfits we were so happy to have before school started in September.

One day at the department store, a man walked behind her counter and helped himself to several blouses. Flabbergasted at his brazenness, my mother politely informed him that if he needed some assistance she would be happy to help him in front of the counter. So impressed was he by her cool headed, non-confrontational manner that he revealed himself as the store owner and gave her a promotion and a raise. Of all things, she became the assistant manager of the complaints department. Can you imagine a shy person spending her days trying to resolve problems with unhappy customers?

To her credit, she was willing to do this job to give us a chance at a good education so we would be prepared to take care of ourselves and not be dependent on anyone else. My mother showed me that you can accomplish that which you think you are not capable of when the need or desire is strong enough.

Like my mother, I never saw myself in business. I really wanted to be a teacher, housewife and mother who created art and did community work on the side. Never in my wildest dreams did I imagine building and sustaining a business for over 25 years.

So here I stand, looking back, living through, and now going forward to carve out a new niche for myself as I turn a corner in my business and my future.

Chapter 3

The Starting Gate

I had been divorced for nearly three years. Working three jobs and being the primary parent raising two kids didn't leave me with a lot free time to date. I thought if I joined one of the popular dating clubs that match people up, I might have a chance at some semblance of a social life.

After two months of hoping and waiting to be selected by an eligible bachelor proved fruitless, it was time for me to become more pro-active. I began reading profiles and making a few choices of my own. No positive responses. I guess being a hard-working, presentable 40-year woman with two school-age children didn't make me the attractive pick I dreamt I might be.

But one man did finally say yes to meeting me. Glenn met me for dessert/coffee at a nearby restaurant one night when my ex husband came to visit the kids. Glenn was gentlemanly and I felt comfortable with him immediately. The best part was that he made me laugh. He had that Mid-Western friendliness and easygoing manner, making him very attractive to me. From our conversation I learned how accomplished and interesting his life to date had been.

He oozed confidence, giving me the impression that he could figure out any problem that came along in life. I learned that he had seven grown children, all sons, and that he was a nuclear engineer and a former

Ventura County supervisor. This was definitely a man of substance and influence.

I didn't know where our conversation over coffee might lead, but I was up for the journey for sure. I had never been out to Moorpark in Ventura County where Glenn lived, even though it's only about a 30-minute ride from my home office in Woodland Hills. I was pleased to find Moorpark a more rural environment with rolling hills and slivers of farmland still being tilled in between tracks of homes. Over the next several months, I became very familiar with the route to his house. I always enjoyed the ride out and the short side trips we used to take in and around Ventura County.

On one of these visits to his home, Glenn was sharing photos of his family with me. His hallway was a literal photo gallery of family members, as was an entire bookcase in his home office. He took great pride in showing me the faces of his growing sons' families with daughters-in-laws and grandchildren.

In one of the photos he was wearing an Air Force uniform. He volunteered that the photo was taken when he was first accepted into the Air Force Academy when he was 18 years old in 1948. I had an OMG moment when I realized he was 18 years older than me. I had figured him to be about 10 years my senior, but not nearly 20 years older. He really didn't look or act his age. His profile didn't mention his age and I wasn't that curious to find out either.

We continued to date and spend time together when my children were with their dad every other weekend. Sometimes I wouldn't see him until after a Saturday night wedding, arriving at his place in Moorpark between 1 and 2 AM very early Sunday morning. We had the next several hours together before I would need to be back home by 5 PM to receive my kids.

Dinner was pre-cooked and saved on the previous Friday before I left for a ceremony rehearsal. This timing routine went on for several months. Occasionally, Glenn and I would have a couple of days together if I had a weekend without a wedding, but it meant I had to often sandwich in introductory and final detail meetings between times with Glenn on these weekends too.

I truly treasured the time Glenn and I spent together. I knew my schedule was not ideal for building a solid relationship. I kept a frenetic schedule, jumping from one business meeting to picking up my daughter, to making it in time for her dance lesson, and still making time to cook dinner for both kids before an evening meeting by 8 PM.

One weekend stands out especially in my memory. We were having lunch on a Saturday afternoon in one of our favorite haunts when Glenn began to ask me a lot of questions about my new wedding business. He was acquainted with my stories of past business ups and downs, so I had a feeling that there was more to these questions than idle chit chat or even sincere interest.

I was about to receive a valuable lesson in life and business I hadn't expected. He started by telling me how, when he was a nuclear engineer working for Rocketdyne, there were times the department he was overseeing was stuck on a solution to a problem; he would stop work and clean house, literally.

He had everyone empty out his or her own desk. Everyone would get boxes and empty out their drawers, throwing out the piles of paper documents that had been taking up space for months without being acted upon. He instructed his staff to clean the tops of their desks and haul away the junk, right down to the candy wrappers stuck in the corners and crevices beneath the paper rubble.

Reorganize, rethink, and reimagine became the mantra and motive for what was essentially a purification ceremony to drive out the demon of non-productive thinking and the malaise that hovered over the department. The team even moved the position of their desks in the room. This exercise was meant to help the group facilitate changes, shaking out the cobwebs while prioritizing the most important tasks in the project at hand.

The next step was drawing a grid on a piece of paper with several lines running from top to bottom and from side to side. The items listed going down would describe the what's of the project and the top of the grid going across the page would be filled in with dates for completion, including deadlines of the coordinating or supportive activities needed to get the job done on time and within budget.

Then he proceeded to do the same thing for my business. I'm thinking holy ***** he's really going to put me through this exercise. He drew a rough grid on a napkin and we started to fill in the blanks as they related to goals and deadlines for the start-up phase of my business. In that one afternoon I learned how to look at the big picture as well as the smaller details that would get me where I wanted to go. I figured out the timing and what actions and tasks needed to be at the forefront to make each segment of my business happen on time and under budget.

I went back to my home office after our lunch with my head spinning, trying to remember everything he had said to help me map out my business operations. Glenn was becoming vested in my success and that was comforting. At the same time I felt nervous that I might not measure up to his standards if I didn't meet the deadlines I proposed.

Deep down I felt Glenn was concerned about my chances of succeeding and he wanted to make sure I would be on solid ground and not be too fanciful about my business.

At the time, my office consisted of my drawing board from my art school days doubling as a desk, a couple of filing cabinets and a hand me down bookcase with at least three layers of paint. I realized that it was time to make a transition to a real desk and equipment to grow and operate a business.

The following week Glenn surprised me by taking me desk shopping and bought me a white Danica wooden desk set with filing drawers and side table to rest my fax machine, copier and daily file folders. He said it had to be a big desk, large enough to use for meetings and spreading out plans, diagrams etc.

Glenn helped me assemble the desk, buy my first proper desk chair and arrange where the furniture should be in the room. Today, someone would have said he was a natural feng shui expert.

I still have that desk, set of drawers and side table. I am so grateful to Glenn for shedding light on the importance of setting measurable goals and having the best equipment you can afford, or in my case gifted. He helped me put the proper ingredients together to support the hours and hours of work and toil that is necessary to initiate a new venture.

His belief in me and the investment he made in helping me set up my office space was invaluable. He helped me see that I was capable, helped me develop a plan, and set the tone and standard for my business for the next 25 years.

Even though our romance stalled when he told me he just didn't want to help raise any more children. I asked him, "How come you got started with me knowing I had school age children?" He said, "I picked you out before you sent a request to meet me, but I never sent the request out because I didn't think you would be interested in me. When I saw your profile, I was so pleased, and said maybe it was meant to be that we should meet."

I was so saddened but I couldn't be mad at him. He had given me so many happy and fun moments. His guidance and caring attitude about my business would leave an indelible mark on my future. I pined away for months after we stopped seeing each other socially and continued to keep in touch. We had become true friends.

When Glenn decided to move out of state, I did visit him for a weekend in Albuquerque, New Mexico the following year. I was wondering if this friendship would develop into a real life version of the movie "Same Time Next Year" where a couple would see each other only once a year, share a long romantic weekend and go their separate ways until the next year. We corresponded by letter and talked over the phone periodically to keep tabs on each other's progress with work and family.

We were having one of our long telephone conversations about five years after we had met when Glenn said, "Well Tobey, if we are both still single and not involved with anyone else when Lauren reaches 18, then perhaps we will get married." That time frame was nearly five years away. I was silent for a second or two trying to really listen to what he was saying to me. The closest he ever got to saying he loved me was one day when I was sitting at his desk years earlier learning how to do something on his computer and he sat down next to me and typed in "I love you". He kissed my left cheek and walked away. He never said those words out loud to me.

Could he really love me still? He admitted that he was selfish and didn't want to change his lifestyle. Perhaps the distance was making his heart grow fonder. Focusing on my head and not my heart, I knew he didn't love me enough to make a commitment or his present life style was more important for him to maintain than to work something out with me and the kids at this juncture. I told him, "Let's just let nature take its course and see what happens".

Perhaps I am being too harsh, but that conversation was tough on me. Even though I wasn't personally being rejected all over again, it was still personal to me since I saw my children and I as a package and not me and my baggage.

As much as I loved and cared for Glenn, I made the decision to accept really letting go this time, feeling there must be a man somewhere in the universe willing to make a commitment to me and my kids without being in a holding pattern for the next five years.

Those five years to follow were filled with business achievements and recognition that made all the hard work and struggle seem worth the sacrifice, but I still longed for a permanent relationship that would culminate in marriage. I had some fun times along the way with a few "what was I thinking" moments that led me down a couple of paths best left in the archives of my memory. I was engaged and unengaged to a Lieutenant of Police too. I didn't lack desire or effort, but I had to face facts that I was in my mid to late forties and the prospect of remarrying was looking pretty grim.

Chapter 4

Fate, Love, and Romance

The beachside air felt a bit toasty for Audrey and Matt's wedding day. Temperatures rose well into the '90s during the day, but by late afternoon the brilliant streaks of coral and turquoise in the sky settled just above the horizon making up for the less-than-ideal climate earlier in the day for this night of romance and love. As with the temperature changing for the better, the rest of the evening would have its stresses and strains early in the evening, but end up being as brilliant and promising as the ceremony sky.

Guests had flown in from all over the United States to witness the mid-summer night's dream celebration. Orchids intertwined with green vines were swaged from row to row of aisle ceremony chairs while tiny fairy lights created a fanciful walk down the aisle for my hopeful bride.

Audrey didn't have many illusions about marriage. She had seen her mom and dad split early in life and had moved several times in the first 18 years of her life. Her mom held the family together from place to place and her father was an infrequent visitor who managed to show up for graduations and birthdays. Still, the allure of having her father walk her down the aisle was important to Audrey. That one gesture would make up for so much in her mind, even if the in between years were lacking his physical and emotional support. For the mother of the bride, however, it was a hard swallow. She felt she had carried a far greater burden without much gratitude from her former spouse.

It was Audrey's wish to put the past in the past and she hoped her parents would do the same. All the planning sessions and conversations to try and make everyone happy were done. It was a relief for Audrey when the wedding day finally arrived, as it was for me as well.

With the pre-ceremony photos finished, the excitement grew as Audrey retired for that last make-up check and a few quiet moments to gather herself before a new chapter in her life would begin.

Within a half an hour, the man of her dreams would take her hand for the first time as her husband. She took a moment in the wedding suite high above their wedding seaside ceremony before she signed the marriage license to write a note to her soon-to-be-husband Matt, and placed it on a bedside table for him to read later that night.

Unlike Audrey, Matt had one set of parents and had lived in the same house until he went away to college. The contrast between Audrey and Matt was striking. Matt's steady and easygoing personality was just what Audrey was looking for to balance her emotional highs and lows. Being a social worker, Matt had a firm grounding in the emotional dynamics of blended families and seemed the perfect mate for Audrey. He was at her side during all the photos and understood why she needed a few minutes of privacy before they signed the marriage license to gather her thoughts.

Guests were beginning to arrive, unconsciously walking in cadence to the classical favorites the tuxedo-clad pianist was playing in the hotel lobby in anticipation of the elegant beachside nuptials.

The ceremony site was adjacent to the hotel's swimming pool, requiring the bride and wedding party to pass the pool to reach the wedding area. The hotel management was confident that by the time the wedding guests began arriving, most hotel guests would have returned to their rooms.

But as the first black-tied and gowned wedding guests made their way to the decorated sun deck, a few bikini-clad guests still lingered by the pool, catching the last rays of daylight.

If my mother had been in my place, she would have given the offending bathers the evil eye, sending them sheepishly back to their rooms. Not being armed with that talent, I began coaxing and cajoling the offenders to make themselves scarce to give the bride a feeling of privacy and privilege for her entrance paralleling the pool.

Within a few minutes the area was empty but for one middle-aged man who continued to float on his back in the middle of the pool like a whale trying to beach itself. He clearly had no intention of honoring my friendly, but impassioned, request to vacate the pool by six o'clock.

My assistants couldn't wait any longer to roll the white cotton runner alongside the outer edge of the pool decking. Audrey envisioned it stretching from the hotel's glass exit doors to the lower deck, creating a 90-foot bridal pathway.

The orchid-laden ceremony arch began reflecting the glow from the garden lights. The nearby palm trees stood like majestic columns framing the back of the aisle as the orange sphere in the sky hung just above the horizon, as if in suspension waiting for Audrey's entrance.

Finally, and to my great relief, the toweled and disgruntled male floater tromped past the waiting bridal party to drier parts unknown.

Audrey stood pensively waiting for her dad to stand next to her for her walk down the aisle. Her dad had already missed most of the pre-ceremony photos creating stress for the photographer and videographer who promised to get shots and footage of Audrey and her father's side of the family before the ceremony. Audrey's father elected to skip that session and slipped in just in time to seat his new fiancée and then double back to walk his daughter down the aisle. Audrey's mom had been the last of the parents to be seated with her second husband and the rest of the wedding party followed.

Once cued, Audrey seemed to glide above the white runner as the strains of Vivaldi's "Spring" filled the air. As Audrey and her father paused at the first row of chairs, her mother stood up, lifted her blusher and kissed her left cheek. Matt came forward shook the hand of the father of the bride and took Audrey's right arm and escorted her forward, just as the evening twilight made its final curtain call.

Audrey and Matt exchanged their vows and sealed their marriage with a kiss as the

string quartet struck up Mendelssohn's "Bridal March". As they exited with wide smiles to the photographer's syncopated flashes, Matt kissed Audrey's cheeks, dampened with tears of joy.

Let the celebration begin!

Most couples decide against a formal receiving line these days, but Audrey and Matt couldn't wait to gather their parents with Best Man and Maid of Honor by their sides to greet everyone in the cocktail area adjacent to the reception room upstairs.

Audrey and Matt raced upstairs to an ante-room off the ballroom to steal away a few moments of privacy, sipping a favorite cocktail they had requested, then shoving a few mouthfuls of hors d'oeuvres down before joining the onslaught of well wishers.

Audrey took a final glance at her compact to check what the seaside humidity had done to her carefully coiffed hair. She removed her veil but kept the borrowed tiara to curb her auburn waves. With her bustle tied underneath her gown, Audrey and her husband made their way into the cocktail area hand in hand. The transition was complete.

They received every hug and kiss with gracious gratitude. Matt's chest was literally bursting, not only with pride but with the many gift envelopes that congratulatory couples pressed into his hands with their good wishes.

The chatter and clatter continued as tray after tray of delicious appetizers came out of the kitchen to disappear in seconds among the hungry guests. Some of the guests lingered in the hallway just outside the ballroom for first dibs on the bite-size gems. Rerouting the culinary treats helped, but these gourmet sniffers followed the aromatic trail wherever it took them, creating a challenge for me to make sure all the guests had a chance to sample the variety of tasty bites.

Once most guests had been greeted and thanked for attending, the receiving line dissolved and the father of the bride approached me with a request to see the bride and groom's wedding night suite. For a second I thought that odd, but I realized that because he didn't see his daughter before the ceremony, he didn't see the room he had paid for his daughter to enjoy for the weekend.

I said, "Sure, no problem, just follow me." As we were about to step into the elevator, he suddenly asked me to hold the door and he dashed off toward the cocktail area. I thought perhaps he had something he wanted to leave in the room like a personal note or gift, so I waited.

It seemed like an eternity, but as soon as the elevator buzzer began to ring, the father of the bride rounded the corner into the elevator with his new fiancée in tow. Arm in arm, they stood beside me almost giddy, giving each other quick kisses one after the other as we made our ascent to the top floor. I just kept looking at the floor numbers flashing as the elevator climbed. It finally dawned on me that this newly engaged couple had more on their minds than simply admiring the lovely bridal suite. I was about to open the door to the suite when the father of the bride snatched the card key away. "I'll take this and return it to you in a few minutes. You must have lots of things to attend to downstairs so you don't have to wait for us."

I took that as my cue to leave, hoping they really would be back shortly. What if Audrey or Matt wanted to go up to their room to freshen up before the grand entrance and found her dad and fiancée enjoying a romantic interlude? Yikes!

Nearly 20 minutes passed when I felt a plastic rectangle being pressed into my left palm. I turned to see the father of the bride and his fiancée passing me on their way to the ballroom, filing in with the other guests to the tunes of the nine-piece orchestra. Thank God the bride and groom hadn't asked me for their room key.

The order of the traditional festivities continued, but the two-to-three-minute toasts that began after the first course morphed into a 15-minute walk down memory lane for the Best Man and Maid of Honor. The pianist began playing softly in the background to encourage the toasters to conclude but the Maid of Honor was oblivious. Finally, the bride and groom stood up, raised their champagne glasses (flat by then), and in unison said, "Thank You" at which point the Maid of Honor finally got the hint and concluded her remarks.

Due to the unexpected long speech by the maid of honor the band members still had to honor the couple's wishes to dance before the main course was served, so the band members had to forego their first break and played to keep the bride and groom happy. I went back in the kitchen to find the Captain for the evening and find out how close we were to serving the next course, the main course. One of the servers told me he couldn't be disturbed. I had nearly 200 people that were getting tired of dancing after nearly 20 minutes and a band that hadn't taken their prescribed break either.

In the kitchen, servers were lined up like pairs of penguins ready to jump off ice cliffs as soon as the plated entrees were ready to serve — but the entrees weren't ready to serve. As it turned out, a large number of guests had requested changes to their entree selection (something that happens more often than I would like to admit). Even though guests had marked their preferences weeks before on their RSVP card, they felt free to make impromptu changes that were causing "service hell" in the kitchen. The staff struggled to meet their wishes, trying to mix and match the entrees they had on hand to satisfy the guests. Audrey's careful entrees per-table tabulation was of little use to the servers by now.

Finally the guests began getting their meals about 30 minutes after the originally scheduled time. I do my best to make sure the band and other service providers are fed while the guests are having their main course so no one loses out on dance music or photo ops. With all the craziness going on in the kitchen over the entrée changes, there was no food prepared for the wedding services. I kept pacing back and forth along the wall of the ballroom parallel to the kitchen trying to think of remedies to make sure the services got food. The hotel's coffee shop was closed by now. I could arrange for pizzas to be brought in, but I knew the hotel wouldn't pay or go for that either.

Three hours into the four-hour dinner reception and the wedding services (photographers, videographers, musicians, etc.) still hadn't received their allocated vendor "bandwiches" (band sandwiches). For some of us it had been nearly nine hours without food.

The band just kept on playing, allowing those guests who had been served to dance, while those guests still eating stayed seated. As entrees were finished, servers' plates navigated the perimeters of the room to avoid collisions with the high-stepping, twirling guests on the dance floor.

The time for the ritual cutting of the cake was drawing near and still no food for the wedding services. I noticed Audrey perspiring something fierce from dancing in her big ball gown. With the cake cutting only five minutes away, she looked me with that, "What am I going to do?" look on her face. I took her into the bathroom for a quick beauty fix, signaling to the band to keep playing; yet another band break lost. By some miracle, Audrey's hair responded well to my efforts and with face powered and lips touched up, we were ready for the cake cutting.

Audrey and Matt were standing over the cake holding the knife in their hands when I spotted Audrey's father and his fiancée slipping out of the ballroom. The father/daughter dance had taken place earlier in the evening so, hopefully, Audrey wouldn't notice her dad missing in action now. I caught up with her father and mentioned we were about to cut the cake. His response, "We will see it in the photos. Thanks anyway."

I couldn't worry about that now. All I could think about was that once the guests sat down to enjoy their cake and coffee, the band would finally be able to eat a little something. I wasn't the only one who was worried about the services. The catering captain felt so badly about the delayed meal service that he put aside the left over regular guests entrees from dinner for the entire wedding team gratis to make up for the late dining.

I came into the kitchen about ten minutes later to tell all the wedding services how grateful I was for their willingness to skip breaks and keep on entertaining the guests. They really saved the pace of the reception. They nodded and kept eating their lukewarm entrees, knowing they would soon have to return to their posts to finish out the night once the guests had finished their cake and coffee.

After the bouquet toss, the last song, and the final hugs and kisses to the bridal party and remaining family from Audrey and Matt, they exited to their penthouse suite. We began gathering our gear trying to put aside all the little glitches that occurred during the day and evening, thinking only about the glow of Audrey and Matt's smiles as they hugged all of us goodnight.

I handed the bandleader an envelope with a tip from the very pleased mother of the bride. I smiled and was turning to get my gear when the bandleader asked me if I was married. Quizzically, I said no. The next question: Was I dating anyone special? No again. The bandleader continued: Would you be interested in meeting someone I think you would like? I said OK. Her final question: How about if I give you a call in a couple of days? I said OK again.

Little did I know, as I casually touched one of the hungry musicians (Bill, the horn player) on the shoulder when thanking them that I was touching my next love interest.

Yes, amid all the doings of the evening, Bill had been watching me traverse the ballroom cuing the families for upcoming toasts, smoothing out service ripples and calming down a nervous bride. The bandleader later told me that at one point in the busy evening he had remarked, "Now that's the kind of woman I could go for." His comment prompted the bandleader to find out my marital status and call me a couple of days later to talk to me about Bill.

Who knows? If the wedding had gone off perfectly without glitches, perhaps Bill wouldn't have had cause to notice me and wouldn't have spoken to the bandleader.

I am an incurable romantic. That's what keeps me going through the rough spots in the planning and execution of a wedding. It just had to be fate that brought us together.

You will have to read a few more chapters to find out what happened with this budding romance :)

Chapter 5

That Special Weekend

You know what I'm talking about — that weekend when you go away for the first time with that special someone for a few days to spend some quality time together without distractions. You get to connect in a way you just haven't been able to make time for. You can be together, just the two of you, twenty-four hours a day, dispensing with work talk or mindless television to fill the gaps in idle moments. This was going to be the kind of weekend that might tell you if this person is a keeper or not.

Here is my version.

Bill and I had been dating exclusively for several months. We hadn't taken any trips, vacations, or getaway weekends together, so I was overjoyed when he made arrangements for us to have a weekend in the Monterey area of Northern California. We had such crazy work schedules — Bill, a trumpeter, music copyist and vocal arranger, and me with my busy wedding planning services, family, and industry activities — that this getaway would be our first chance to slow down enough to become closer.

His sister had mentioned a great bed and breakfast inn in Monterey that sounded just perfect. Turn-of-the-century architecture, bay windows overlooking the Pacific Ocean, complimentary breakfast, sitting rooms, late-afternoon gathering with libations...you get the picture.

I was so used to planning events for my clients that it was a welcome change to have someone else take care of the details. My assistant in the office would check my messages while I was away, allowing me to take those deep breaths that are so necessary as another busy event season comes to a close in early December.

We decided to take Pacific Coast Highway (PCH), the coastal route that promised terrific views while allowing us to visit Bill's parents on a Thursday night in Santa Barbara before leaving for Monterey the next morning. They lived in a retirement community with individual cottages and duplexes. When we arrived, Marialice and Paul were so gracious, insisting we take their bedroom for the night. We enjoyed a hearty dinner in the community dining room, sparing them the effort of having to cook for us.

In the morning as we prepared to leave, we listened to weather reports that predicted moderate rain and wind, dashing our hopes for a brilliant sunny drive up the coast. We considered turning back or taking an alternate inland route, but in the end we decided to stick with the coast, even if the views might be a bit gray and foggy. Actually, the thought of driving past white crested waves on one side of the highway while hunter green coastal pines hugged us on the other seemed romantic and infinitely preferable to the dried-out landscape of Los Angeles in late fall.

We were definitely up for it, anticipating a quaint fireplace at the end of the day warming us as we gazed out the bay window at the surf pounding the jagged rocks below. What a perfect respite from a hectic wedding season.

We left Marialice and Paul's at nine Friday morning, leaving plenty of time to reach Monterey by nightfall. Our plan was to stop for lunch along the way at Nepenthe Restaurant, quite famous for being the home that Orson Wells built for fabled film star, Rita Hayworth.

We were only about thirty minutes outside of Santa Barbara when the windshield wiper housing on the driver's side collapsed and disappeared into the cavity at the bottom of the windshield. We pulled into the first gas station we saw where a local mechanic finagled a repair in less than 15 minutes; a minor mishap until Bill reached for his wallet and realized he had left it in his leather jacket in his folk's closet. Luckily, I had enough money to pay for the windshield wiper repair. We turned around and drove back to Santa Barbara to retrieve Bill's jacket and wallet and headed out again. Ugh!

Having lost more than an hour over the wiper episode, we realized that we might not make it to Monterey before nightfall. The weather report had worsened and now called for increasing heavy rain with possible mudslides along (US 1). That meant we might have to take the inland route, a detour that would have nixed our lunch at Nepenthe. For miles on our way to Santa Barbara Bill had listened to me talk up the historic house that was now Nepenthe restaurant, not to mention the food, especially their savory tuna burgers.

Listening to the discouraging weather reports on the car radio didn't make me any happier. But Bill was by nature more adventuresome than I, so we stayed the course on (US 1), hoping to reach both Nepenthe and Monterey before nightfall.

As we approached the final bridge before Nepenthe, the fog rolled in making driving precarious, at best. Small rock and soil spills from the hillsides started accumulating on the right side of the road. I sat on my hands rocking back and forth trying not to appear more anxious than I was feeling. Approaching the next curve, we encountered flashing caution lights warning that the road would narrow to a single lane ahead. We realized there hadn't been another car in front of us on the road for miles and we now both feared that the local authorities were about to turn us back.

We got lucky. The men in the yellow rain gear waved us on. We soon realized we were the last car allowed to pass before the "closed road" sign was posted behind us.

We arrived at Nepenthe minutes later, still giddy at our good luck. The place was packed, but we were able to get one of the last tables. Happily sheltered from the fog and intermittent rain, we sat down and studied our menus leisurely while taking in the ambience.

A fifty-foot bar made of wood and red leather lined the restaurant's back wall.

Opposite what seemed like a hundred feet of glass windows overlooked the steep majestic cliffs above the Pacific Ocean.

I ordered the famous savory tuna burger that had been on my mind for the last 200 miles and it wasn't hard to convince Bill to try one too. The only open table was right in the middle of the room. Since the view was partially obscured by the fog, we weren't missing much. As we were seated, I noticed a black plastic container near my right foot the size of a litter box. I was thinking maybe a server inadvertently left a dishpan while bussing tables.

When the rain started up again, I realized that the container was there to catch the water leaking from above. We did a pretty good job of ignoring the drops pinging into the pail as we sat and talked.

Minutes after taking our order, our waiter returned to regretfully inform us that the kitchen had only one tuna burger left. Wanting Bill to experience the culinary delicacy I was so enthused about, I opted for one of their juicy beef burgers instead. We kept telling each other how thankful we were to have made it this far and how hopeful we were for a smoother-running weekend to come.

We rolled into Monterey amid clearing skies just as the sun was beginning to set. Soon we spotted the seven gables peaking above the cypress pines surrounding the old Victorian mansion. As soon as we parked we grabbed our luggage and announced ourselves at the quaint front desk only to find that our room was still occupied.

Somehow our room had been double booked and the innkeeper apologized and asked us if we would take another small room at a reduced rate for the first night. In the morning they would move us as soon as the room was cleaned. They also offered us a voucher for the chance to book elsewhere for that first night, but at that point we were just thrilled to have a bed in which to rest our weary bones and not have to get back into the car and take a chance at another location.

We tromped up to the third floor to a charmingly petite attic room with a small corner window, giving us a quick peek at the ocean minutes before the sun went down. Finding space for his photo equipment was Bill's top priority. With his camera bag still on his right shoulder, he swung around quickly to his left looking for a closet, barely missing a fragile milk-glass lamp and a table to his right. I had just enough time to shield the white silk shade, or we would have had a floor littered with glass shards.

Finding room for our clothes was another matter. Bill set his equipment and clothes inside the small cupboard just left of the doorway, not realizing that it was the room's only vertical space, leaving just about one foot's width of room for both of us to hang our clothes. With the closet filled, I decided to just leave my belongings in my suitcase next to the milk-glass lamp and table. After all, we were only going to spend one night in this hyper-cozy Victorian room.

I was gathering my toiletries when Bill called out in an alarming tone, "Tobey, you've got to see this in the bathroom." What now, I thought, taking the two paces to the bathroom while ducking under the slanted roofline to my right. Bill turned to me with a Santa Claus-face of shaving cream, holding up a razor and demanding to know how he was supposed to shave when the pedestal sink was placed two feet to the right of the antique wall mirror. At this point the only words that came out of my mouth were, "Where there's a will, there's a way," followed by, "Let's just figure we are camping in a fancy tent."

The next morning was more hopeful. The sky was filled with those white puffy clouds storks fly through on commercials. Our room would be ready right after we finished the country breakfast that awaited us downstairs. As we entered the common area Bill said something that made it apparent that he had never stayed in bed and breakfast inn before. He asked the innkeeper to direct us to our reserved table for breakfast. The innkeeper smiled nervously and informed him that everyone sits at the big table in the dining room and to just pick a spot and breakfast would be served shortly. I knew Bill wasn't a big morning person, but his silence seemed deafening to the rest of us. Reluctantly, he participated in the morning banter with the other guests. I was beginning to learn just how much a creature of habit Bill was and I could see that it wasn't easy for him to switch gears and be talkative in the morning. Since I'm the opposite and have a sunny disposition in the morning, I began thinking I sure hope there won't be too many more of these incompatible traits to discover about Bill.

After the last few gulps of coffee, the rest of the day would surely go smoother than our start. We got situated into our new room and had a great day ahead of us that included a tour of the Monterey Aquarium, followed by a visit to the migrating monarch butterfly haunts. We also had the pleasure of anticipating a great seafood dinner at one of the famed Monterey restaurants.

Years before, Bill's sister had dated the director of the aquarium and was able to arrange a personal tour that was just fascinating. We were taken to see the back holding tanks for aquatic life and learned so much about how the staff works with sea life conservation and preservation.

Then we moved on to the butterfly forest where Bill was intent on photographing one of their yearly migration havens. Camera gear in hand, we hiked into the preserve and found at least 100,000 sleeping monarchs, their wings folded together behind them. It looked like a thick layer of light brown leaves was smothering the fifty-foot trees. They were just not ready to wake up and display their vibrant orange, gold and black wings. After two hours of scouting around for any awakening butterflies, we scuttled the mission.

We channeled our disappointment into pure fascination at how their homing instinct brings these beautiful winged insects together year after year to the same grove of trees.

Arriving back at our comfy haven at the inn, we changed our clothes for the evening relishing the great dinner to come. The restaurant was within walking distance, and we planned to come back to our room and enjoy a romantic evening in front of the wood-burning fireplace.

At the restaurant we selected the same entrée: white fish, mashed potatoes and sautéed spinach, and it was delicious. Unfortunately, about two hours later back at the inn, in front of a roaring fire, we both began to feel nauseated. The fish dinner we had looked forward to all day left us in a state of gastronomic distress.

After taking turns in the bathroom for the next few hours, we finally fell asleep about two in the morning. We slept in and missed breakfast, which neither of us could have eaten anyway.

I decided to stay in for the early part of the day, resting and reading on the comfy antique couch in front of the bay window overlooking the ocean. Bill, feeling more peppier than I, gathered his photography gear and ventured across the street to the rock formations just above the ocean to shoot the crashing waves swallowing the jagged rocks in their foam. I caught a glimpse of him as he leaned over the rocks facing the ocean to get as close as he could to the swirling, glistening sprays of water as they landed on the rocks below.

After an hour of reading I felt groggy and set my glasses down on the arm of the couch and drifted off to sleep in the soft down cushions. With my book on my chest, I awakened to a knock on the door. It was Bill back from his watery photographic adventure. He came around to my comfy perch on the sofa and leaned over to give me a big kiss before sitting down next to me. The only problem was he decided to sit down on the arm of the couch, right where I had placed my reading glasses. A crunching sound followed by "OMG, I didn't see the glasses," interrupted my quiet morning rest. I managed a wimpy smile and said, "It's okay." I had opted for thin frames glasses that blended into the muted taupe and sandalwood colored couch; no wonder Bill didn't see them.

With my cockeyed glasses held together with a rubber band, we grabbed lunch in town and then decided to take the famous 17-Mile Drive in Carmel, a ritual for tourists visiting the central coast. Slowly, we followed the road as it meandered through a section of the Pebble Beach Golf Course, enjoying the magnificent beach homes and the wind-sculpted pine trees that lined the road.

After the drive Bill grabbed his camera and we headed to the beach to make the most of the golden light before sunset. Bill was in his element capturing images of the low tide and webbed-footed trails in the sand. Particularly interesting were the small tidal pools that reflected the striated clouds above. I was watching him take photos for about thirty minutes when Bill realized that he had put the wrong film in the camera. You are right, we are talking old school film cameras. I offered to jog a quarter mile back to the car to swap out the film canisters. I really wasn't being gracious here. It was really my way of working off some calories so I could have dessert that night. I just felt badly that he may have lost some great images with the sunlight diminishing the opportunity to catch the best light before sundown.

Mission accomplished, I returned in time for Bill to capture what he was after earlier. We strolled back to Bill's car to return to our vintage nest for a second and, hopefully, healthier night together. A mile or two en route we both heard a horrendous noise coming from outside the car. We turned off the radio to listen closer but couldn't figure out where the clanging, grinding noise was coming from. Even though Bill's decade-old Peugeot wagon had seen nearly 200,000 miles, he babied it through regular engine tune-ups, so it had to be something he just couldn't have foreseen.

He pulled over and asked me to get out of the car so I could tell him if there was something loose or dragging below the car. The noise just had to be coming from outside the car. As I stood on the curb watching him make a few passes in front of me, I couldn't hear a thing nor could I see anything hanging from the car. I kept thinking how bizarre this whole experience was becoming. I climbed back into the car and told Bill I couldn't hear a thing. The disbelief on his face seemed to indicate that he thought I must be hard of hearing. If I knew how to drive a stick shift I would have offered to take the wheel so he could make his own observations. We decided to drive slowly to the nearest gas station to see if they could figure out what demons were lurking in Bill's aging, beloved metal and glass chariot.

After a few minutes of review, the mechanic came to the conclusion that the lug nuts on the housing of the wheels were so worn from so many years of tire changes and rotations that the threads on the screws could no longer grab anything, causing the loud, clanging noise when driving.

What to do? Since the car was an older foreign model, our only option was to order new lug nuts from a factory back east and, hopefully, by the time we arrived safely back to LA, we could expect them in the mail by Monday or Tuesday. The mechanic found four used lug nuts the same size as the ones on the car and put one good lug nut on each of the four wheels. He assured us that if we drove slowly in the right lane back to LA, the loose three lug nuts on each wheel would not present a real threat to our safety. He followed that statement with, "But if you hear any strange noises, pull over immediately and call the Auto Club."

When we finally pulled into my driveway early on Sunday evening we both heaved a big sigh of relief, shook our heads and exchanged a knowing smile — the weekend was not exactly what we had planned, but we were stronger for it because we shared the ups and downs together.

Well, you will have to read on to find out how Bill and I finally got together forever and ever. Just as with our trip to Monterey, we had some unexpected twists and turns in our road to matrimony.

Chapter 6

I Didn't Want to be a Great Date Forever

One autumn night after Bill and I had been dating for a good year I decided the time had come for me to find the courage to ask him what his long-term intentions were towards me. He had never once approached the subject, leaving me to be the one to bring it up, even though I dreaded a negative outcome.

We were sitting at my kitchen table having coffee and dessert when I asked him where he felt we were going, now that we had been dating for a year. He glanced downward at his coffee cup and said, "You know how I am. I'm used to living alone and there hasn't been anyone significant in my life for quite a while."

That comment spoke volumes to me. I realized in an instant that he didn't want to move the relationship forward, even if he loved me the way he said he did. So I just blurted out, "Bill, I don't want to be just a great date for the rest of my life."

I leaned in. "I get it that you are comfortable with the way things are between us but I want more. And since I believe you are serious when you say you don't want to change our relationship, I want you to know that I am going to make myself available to date other men, even if that means I will lose you, because ultimately I won't be happy in the future if our relationship doesn't progress."

I could hardly believe I was able to say those words. My knees were shaking under the table, but I knew I couldn't stay in the same holding pattern much longer. I could have really blown it with Bill, but I felt I deserved to be totally happy and if Bill didn't see me as a potential wife, I would only grow resentful if I spent years waiting for him to come around.

"I don't want to stand in your way to find complete happiness," was Bill's reply.

I said, "Okay, I just wanted you to know I met a rabbi through my business and he has asked me out to lunch. I have a feeling he is interested in me in a social way too and I wanted to let you know before I accept his invitation." Still no change in Bill's response; S***, this was going to be tough!

Sure enough, I went to lunch with the rabbi and while he was charming and fun to be with, I was still pining away for Bill. My feelings weren't like a faucet that I could turn off and on at will. If I took Bill literally, I had to try to turn the page and begin a new chapter in my love life.

Meanwhile, the rabbi was pursuing me like crazy. He asked me to read the sermon he was working on for High Holy days. I attended High Holy Days at his synagogue and was given the honor of opening the arc (the cabinet that holds the Torahs during the service). I began building a relationship with Rabbi Josh.

Finally, a good month after I started dating the rabbi, Bill called me with the news that he wanted to make a serious lifetime commitment to me. He said he understood that his words alone might not be convincing because he had backed off once before and now there was someone new in my life. He told me to take my time deciding, that he would fight for me. Wow, what a turnaround.

This is the part where you might expect me to say I jumped with joy at the news that Bill missed me and wanted to make a real commitment. But the truth is, Bill had hurt me deeply when he rejected me and I really didn't trust that his feelings were genuine. I wanted to believe him, but I had finally started to feel comfortable around Rabbi Josh. Now, in all good conscience, I had to bring Rabbi Josh up to date as to where my situation stood with Bill. As you can imagine, Rabbi Josh wasn't thrilled about Bill's change of heart, but he didn't bolt. Believe it or not, I continued to see both Bill and Rabbi Josh casually for the next three months.

Bill and I would go to movies and dinners, while Rabbi Josh and I would take dance lessons, fix things around my home and have homemade dinners. Each of them faxed me love notes every few days as they vied for my attention. You'd think I would have basked in the attention of two competing suitors, but it was really quite stressful, especially when the three of us ended up working the same weddings. I would dash about handling details while Rabbi Josh performed the ceremonies and Bill played in the reception orchestra. It got to the point where Rabbi Josh wanted to move closer to me so we could spend more time together.

I just couldn't manage this triangle relationship much longer. Conflicted, I spoke with a counselor and — believe it or not — a graphology specialist too. The counselor and handwriting specialist each confirmed what I had sensed about our individual characteristics, quirks, and personalities. None of the three of us were without flaws, but what mattered was that I first recognize my own set of idiosyncratic tendencies. Then I could determine whether Rabbi Josh or Bill — each with his own set of characteristics — would be the most compatible mate. This process guided me to a decision.

Finally I recognized that no matter how much I had in common with the older, taller, handsome and intelligent Rabbi Josh, I still loved Bill...Bill who was shorter than me, not of the same religion and certainly not handy around the house. Still, we shared the same brand of caring and attachment to family along with compatible morals, values, and priorities. Bottom line, I had been in love with Bill all along.

I know that if I had never known Bill I could have been happy with Rabbi Josh with his many admirable qualities: He was an inspired leader, talented in languages, artistic, and even had a lovely singing voice. I really looked up to him, but my heart belonged to Bill.

Several months had passed since Bill said he would fight for me. On New Year's Day (1997)Bill and I were having dinner with a couple of his close friends. I turned to him while our friends were in the kitchen getting some coffee cups for us and I said that if the offer to get married is still in his heart, I would take him up on it. We laughed, hugged and kissed.

How to break the news to Rabbi Josh? I called him on the phone about the beginning of the second week in January after Bill and I set the date of November 29, 1997. I told Rabbi Josh that Bill had made a lifetime commitment to me. As expected, Rabbi Josh didn't believe Bill would really go through with marriage because he knew Bill was nearing 55 years of age and hadn't been married before.

In the end, Rabbi Josh proposed that we set a lunch date one year from the day we first had lunch together, about four months away. "If you show up," he said, "I'll know you are no longer with Bill and that you will commit to me. If you don't show up, I'll know you and Bill are getting married."

I didn't meet him for lunch.

Bill and I were married in my backyard before a group of our oldest friends and family by a rabbi friend we met through business. Bill's father, a retired American Baptist minister, assisted in the ceremony. As part of the ceremony, Bill's dad read letters we had written to each other saying why we wanted to marry the other. Bill's letter was touching and romantic. Then Bill's dad read my letter. I don't know if it was the way he read it, but everyone started to laugh and I realized that my quirky sense of humor had unintentionally crept into my sincere sentiments about Bill. That would have been enough of a surprise on our wedding day, but the very bandleader who had been responsible for getting us together in the first place surprised us by showing up and singing a love song to us during our ceremony.

After our backyard ceremony under the Fruitless Mulberry tree, our 60 guests migrated to the kitchen and the adjoining outside deck while the catering company set up the dinner tables on our grassy lawn. To entertain our guests while the backyard was being repositioned, Bill, his brother David and his dad Paul sang tunes in three-part harmony recalled from summer vacations spent on their grandparents' Kansas farm.

Soon the backyard was transformed into a cozy fall garden with tree lanterns and trellis lights intermingling with hanging clusters of grapes still clinging to their autumn vines above the covered patio. In the crisp, clear California November air the lights sparkled like a crown cresting our hill-top house.

We didn't realize just how visible our wedding lights must have been from above the normally dark streets around us. A small plane kept buzzing back and forth making half a dozen passes during our wedding. We don't live in an exclusive area for sure, but our festive lighting definitely attracted attention.

We didn't have to worry about the noise level from our DJ since our closest neighbors were also friends with whom we had lived side by side for more than 20 years. We were also blessed with perfect weather. We had endured three solid days of rain before the sun broke through for our wedding day. The rain then commenced the following afternoon.

It's hard to believe that over seventeen years have passed since our wedding day. Traveling with Bill is still interesting and, believe it or not, he has become handier around the house. My love and respect for him as a person has not diminished. I am one lucky gal.

Epilogue: A few years after Bill and I got married, my Aunt Ethel and Uncle Seymour decided to have a commitment ceremony and party for their fiftieth wedding anniversary. We offered our backyard, but Uncle Seymour's health had deteriorated, and since it would be a summer celebration, we opted for an air- conditioned banquet room rather than a steamy-hot valley backyard.

As the date approached I got a call from my cousin Julie asking my opinion on the set up for the ceremony. She told me the rabbi had requested a small table and lavalier mic. She asked me to explain what a lavalier mic was and I asked her out of curiosity who was going to perform the recommitment ceremony. You guessed it: Rabbi Josh. I started to laugh because my cousins hadn't known the name of the rabbi I had been seeing before Bill and I got engaged. When I explained it to Julie, I heard a sharp gasping sound on the other end of the line. I told her no worries; everything would be just fine. It turns out that

Rabbi Josh was recommended by the banquet center they selected for the celebration.

On the day of Aunt Ethel and Uncle Seymour's anniversary celebration, I knew Rabbi Josh and I would cross paths. It was going to be awkward with Bill and myself there as a married couple, but I was hopeful that Rabbi Josh would be happy in his life and that I would have receded to a minor footnote in his life.

I found Rabbi Josh checking the set up in the banquet room before the guests were seated. I brought Bill with me to the ceremony room and introduced Bill to Rabbi Josh. Rabbi Josh was gracious and friendly. Bill decided to give us a few minutes alone to catch up and reminisce. It was good that we had a chance to talk face to face after everything that went down. Rabbi Josh seemed content in his life. He was traveling, doing speaking engagements and conducting holiday services on cruise ships in the Caribbean.

For those few moments, I felt like we were just two old friends catching up with each other. We traded compliments and shared what we were doing professionally. He let me know that he was in a committed relationship and that made me happy.

Looking back now, I know that if I had been asked to choose between Bill and Rabbi Josh based on written profiles, I would have gravitated toward the Rabbi's. But a profile on paper is just that, a listing of the facts and figures of someone's life statistics, but not the heart, soul, and chemistry you feel when you are with them.

Chapter 7

My Own Wedding Day Blunder

By the time Bill and I married in 1997, I had been coordinating and dispensing wedding wisdom for at least nine years. With more than three hundred weddings under my belt, I had a high opinion of my ability to solve most issues that come up in a diplomatic and sensitive manner. Surely I wasn't going to do something foolish or improper in the planning or execution of my wedding day.

Well, I'm here to tell you that no one is immune to awkward moments, faux pas, or off putting remarks, even if you are supposed to know what you are doing. It's just human nature to sometimes become inflexible and narrow minded because you think you are being fair, but not all rules of etiquette are followed all the time and sometimes for good reasons.

I know not every guideline can be followed exactly, but I do my best to apply my version of the fairness doctrine across the board, thinking that doing so is the right way to operate in life. Fair is fair, right? I'm not so sure now!

I never considered the personal cost of trying to be fair all the time. I could plead insanity, ignorance, or diminished capacity, but none of that would be true. I was so focused on one moment - the wedding day - which I didn't consider the long-term effects of one myopic decision. What follows is my account of how in the process of managing my own small wedding with limited resources; I witnessed a friendship of nearly 15 years collapse.

When planning my wedding with Bill, we had a heart-to-heart talk about how many people we should invite and would actually fit in our backyard. We have a striking view of the San Fernando Valley, but a postage-stamp size grass area in our backyard. We measured, imagined, and finally figured out that we could squeeze in four tables on the outside lawn and move the family room furniture into the garage and fit three 48-inch round tables seating a total of 24 people inside the house for a total of 60 guests, including us.

To be perfectly honest, I would have loved to have had a bigger wedding and pull out all the stops, but the reality was, we had three children between us with one in college and two with college on the horizon. We both decided that sixty was the magic number of guests we could invite given our space and budget. Then we had to figure out who could be shoehorned into our bulging guest list of sixty-four sans children.

Where do you draw the line between immediate and extended family? Since neither of us had large families, we felt we could also invite our oldest and dearest friends if some of our extended family members might decide not to come, since our wedding fell on the Saturday following Thanksgiving. We eliminated children except for the two children of my first cousins acting as flower girl and ring bearer. The squeeze came when some of our friends expected to bring their children along too. After all, we knew some of our friends' children from before they were born. Even the neighbors I had lived side by side with for nearly 25 years had children who had grown up playing with my children. This situation was getting tougher and tougher by the minute.

As one of my closest friends, Cindy left me most conflicted about my decision to only have two children present besides our own three. With Cindy's three children and all the other friends' children, we were looking at potentially a good 80 guests. We knew we didn't have the room for that, so I drew a firm line in the sand and said no kids other than the flower girl and ring bearer.

I probably took the easy way out, but I felt that if for some reason a few guests weren't able to come, by all means we could invite some of the kids along closer to the wedding day.

From my years in business, I knew that the smaller the wedding, the less likely it was that guests would drop out. In the end, we invited sixty-six guests thinking we would get sixty yeses. Well, I might have been right about the numbers, but I was dead wrong about what would happen next.

Since more of my family was local and able to attend and several of Bill's extended family couldn't make it, I thought it fair to have Bill invite more of his close friends. That left fourteen guests for Bill and nine for me. I had gotten to know most of his friends through Bill's music business, but I hadn't spent much quality time with them. I was hopeful that the wedding day would be a time we could get to know each other a little better.

I just didn't imagine that six of Bill's fourteen friends would not stay through dinner. Two left right after the ceremony because they had to get to a music gig, but they never let us know that before the wedding day. Four additional friends of Bill's stayed through the cocktail hour and then went on to other events. We ended up with one empty table in the family room. I felt awful. If only I had known about the possibility of early departures, I could have had Cindy's children come and a few other children with whom I had become especially close over the years.

The damage was done. I just tried to put a good face on, but in my heart I felt so badly for Cindy and for me too. I knew I had disappointed her terribly. Our friendship was never the same after the wedding. We had a chance to see each other at a group dinner with her temple friends, but when I had an event on the same day as her second daughter's bat mitzvah and had to decline the invitation, that was the last straw. I had lost a close confidant and friend.

When I became a single parent and my kids just needed a place to land and know they were in safe and caring hands, Cindy was there for me, especially when I had business circumstances that took me away for several hours unexpectedly. Dancing lessons for the kids, scores of birthday celebrations shared, along with secrets and dreams, forged close ties that should have stood the test of time if I had had more forethought.

I learned not all in life should be decided on what seems fair and reasonable. Sometimes special relationships have to be honored not for what seems fair, but more for what is valued and cherished. Even though I have been able to forgive my shortsightedness, I will always regret the loss and any hurt I caused Cindy and her family.

Years later, I had a turn of events which gave me a personal flashback to Cindy's feelings, only this time I was the one with hurt feelings. My dear nephew got married and he and his partner decided to surprise their parents by not telling them ahead of time that they were getting married. My nephew knew that the parents would probably want the close relatives to be included and would have exercised their voices to a high degree over this decision to have a very private gathering with just their close friends as witnesses to the nuptials.

They decided to have a courthouse wedding ceremony and my sister and brother-in-law had no idea until the day of the wedding. They were overjoyed to see their son and his partner get married. Their son and partner made all the arrangements themselves.

Their decision to only include a close circle of friends and their parents was a very private decision. They knew there might be some criticism that would follow. It must have been a very difficult decision for sure.

Following the courthouse wedding ceremony the newlyweds had their gourmet dinner as the focus of their wedding reception. They rented a private dining room in one of Los Angeles's nicest restaurants and pulled out all the stops. Several courses with paired wines and unbelievable desserts plus a simple wedding cake was the planned bill of fare for the evening for the fourteen guests attending.

When I saw the photos and heard the news from my sister, I was thrilled for them both, but so disappointed I couldn't witness their wedding ceremony. I really didn't care about the dinner for myself and then I remembered those exact words coming from Cindy nearly 16 years earlier. She told me her kids just wanted to see us get married and staying for dinner wasn't important to her children.

I had to do some soul searching now. I knew in my heart my nephew would never do anything intentional to hurt any of his family.

No one else in the family talked about the extended family not attending. For all I know I was the only one who felt slighted. I wasn't thinking about anyone else but myself at that moment.

Knowing that the newlyweds had the wedding they wanted and are happily married is very important to me. They were together for twelve years before they got married. Their wedding day ultimately should have been the way they wanted it to be. I want to believe the disappointment I felt and the conversation that followed with my nephew was an honest reaction shared, and even though a bit awkward for me, it was much better than harboring repressed feelings that would wound an important relationship for both of us in the future.

I've tried to bring the lessons I learned from this personal experience by sharing, when appropriate, with my clients to help them through some emotional lightning strikes of their own making.

Too often logic or reliance on formalities overrides true feelings and priorities are clouded as a result. Sometimes one needs to make decisions because it feels right, even when it may be perceived as selfish or shortsighted.

In my case, if I had to do it over again, I would have invited Cindy's children for the ceremony and then they could have stayed on when those guests suddenly left after cocktails. Perhaps some other friends might have been miffed, but there's no going back now. It's when you experience awkward moments regarding etiquette issues you learn the importance of being true to your inner feelings and core values to guide you in making your decisions rather than blind allegiance to outside social norms or pressures.

Chapter 8

Bill's Lost and Found Wedding Ring

A few years back I read a story about a lost wedding band and how a group of well-meaning citizens came together to buy this newlywed another ring. It brought a smile to my face, but also a grimace as I recalled our own lost wedding band saga, a tale less dewy with newlywed bliss but all the more fortified with marital strength and endurance.

When we picked out our wedding bands together, we wanted them to share a common motif symbolizing our special bond. The result was a twisted rope detail in my band that was mirrored by a braided design in his. His large knuckles left the ring a little loose around the base of his ring finger, but we thought that his knuckle would prevent the ring from slipping off. The jeweler agreed.

After we had been married about four years Bill was taking a test in a mobile medical van and was asked to remove all metal objects. He deposited his ring, wallet and watch in a drawer next to the examining room. Yes you guessed it — when the test was over he opened the drawer, retrieved his wallet and watch, and rushed back to his office to make a deadline sans the wedding ring, which must have slipped into a back corner of the drawer where it wasn't easily seen.

I wasn't happy that night when I pointed out that he must have left it in the drawer. I rolled my eyes, and said something like, "You didn't notice you weren't wearing your ring"? I sighed deeply and tried not to take it personally. The next day he called the company that supplied the medical testing van, but the ring was not found.

Life goes on. We started saving and two years later we purchased a replacement ring, thinking this ring will be the final one. But a couple of years later on a Thanksgiving weekend my husband went to the airport to pick up his daughter and had another mishap. While there he used the bathroom, washed his hands and exited without the hard-earned replacement ring. The original scenario repeated itself when he got home and he realized it must have slipped into a paper towel and then into the wastebasket while drying his hands. He called the airport's lost and found department, but to no avail. I won't share what I said to him when he lost the ring for the second time.

At this point, you must be thinking that Bill has a subliminal motive for letting his wedding rings stray. He, however, surmised that it was because he married for the first time at age 55 and wasn't accustomed to wearing rings. OK, okay excuse my cockeyed optimism, but I believed him. With gold prices on the rise, we decided perhaps it would be best to forego another ring, accept the loss and go on.

About two years later I arrived a little early at the Glendale Shopping Galleria where I was meeting a friend for lunch. It was near Valentine's Day and of course I strolled by the jewelry counter "just to look" when a diminutive, elderly lady stood beside me and said, "which ring do you like?"

"The one on the left," I said smiling.

To my surprise, she swung around the counter, unlocked the cabinet and out came the box and ring. I was stunned for a moment. The friendly shopper I thought I was talking to turned out to be an earnest saleswoman wanting to know what I thought of the ring.

I apologized for taking her time up, explaining I was just window-shopping before a lunch date. But suddenly I was spilling out the story of how my husband had lost two rings and I kept hoping someday I might be able to purchase another one that would actually stay on his finger.

"You know, dear," she said intently, "If you really like this ring, it's worth getting because it's on sale and, frankly, that particular design won't be here again."

I don't know if I just got caught up in Valentine's Day hearts and flowers or what, but she gave me another discount on top of the sale and away I went, pretty gift bag in hand wondering how I was going to pay this ring off before the interest on my credit card would negate the savings I had just scored. Okay this should have been the end of the story. Wife gets ring, husband is grateful, and they live happily ever after.

Well the happy part is true, but we are not finished with the ring. I sauntered out the glass doors of JC Penny's stowing the gift bag containing the "trinket" in my oversized red leather purse. My friend called me on my cell phone to say she was going to be a little late. No problem, I just set my purse on the concrete bench in front of me and waited, glowing in the aftermath of my great fortune while desperately hoping this ring which was a little wider and thicker than the others, would stick with its owner.

I was looking toward the street for my friend Pam when I felt this big push in the middle of my back. Before I could turn around, I found myself tumbling over the concrete bench and onto the concrete sidewalk below looking up at the sky. The only thing on my mind was that I'd been mugged and someone got the ring. I rolled over and was struggling to my feet when a UPS driver rushed over, exclaiming that he didn't see me (all five foot, ten of me) when he hit me from behind. Purse and ring intact I regained my composure. Fortunately, he had hit me with a large flat-bed cart stacked with boxes too high to see around instead of his four-thousand pound truck. Seconds later Pam arrived, and after sorting out the insurance details, we had tea and a bite of lunch. I needed a few minutes to gather myself and figure out if I could drive or not. My left arm was really hurting so I decided to drive home, give my husband the ring and go to the hospital to get checked out. No hero here, just stubborn enough to tough it out until I got to the hospital. I was banged up, sore, and with my left arm questionable as to a fracture; another appointment was needed the next day with a specialist. The long and short of it was I got better over time, my husband had his ring and he was really grateful I was okay.

Now this really should have been the end of the story. Well not to bore you, but… another couple of years went by and my husband had arranged to meet a colleague to pick up some original music score sheets. They met up the coast at a small airport that has a nice little coffee shop. And yes, he managed to lose the third wedding ring even though it was thicker around. This time he noticed his ring was missing that evening when he was washing his hands before dinner at home.

By now you must be thinking that this is either the cleanest man on earth and you will never catch a cold from him, or that he is the most absent-minded, non-observant son of a gun who ever lived. I'm not weighing in on that one either.

I looked at him after he told me this third tale of woe and said, "okay no more rings. I'm done." He drove back up to the small airport early the next morning, rushed into the cafe and asked if they had emptied the bathroom trash cans yet. One of the employees said yes, but the garbage truck hadn't come around to empty the bin, so the ring might still be retrievable. My husband climbed into the smelly trash bin while the employee identified the bags that came from the bathroom. Sure enough, the ring was in the garbage. Subsequently, we had the ring sized down to the point where it will be extremely hard to ever take off, wash off…you get the idea.

If you knew Bill and me, you would know this story is true. We both have been through enough in our lives to know what is important and what is forgivable. No mysteries or intrigue here. Just two souls with some wear and tear on their soles that trust each other and have learned that sometimes you just have to say, "What happened today, dear?" pass the butter and chew.

Chapter 9

My First Unofficial Assistant

At the end of each year I invite my assistants over to my house for a thank you dinner. It's my way of showing my appreciation for all their hard work throughout the past year. If it weren't for their keen eyes and good instincts, many of my weddings would not have run as smoothly as they did.

Their extra care has made all the difference to me and I know my clients feel the same way once they experience the level of care and attention my assistants provide. Even though they are independent contractors, they treat each of my clients as if they were family.

At our yearly dinners we talk about the year that was, what we might have done differently, what we hope for the next, and lessons learned.

Usually for this dinner I break out my fine crystal, silver, and china and do it up right for my honored guests. But last year I decided to do something different. I still felt the same way about them, but I wanted to do something off script. I decided on a "bowl night" with lots of colorful small bowls for each course, creating a friendly and fun buffet-style dinner rather than a formal plated dinner.

I was preparing earlier in the day of our dinner when I retrieved a copper serving bowl from the top shelf in the pantry. Sitting inside was an old Polaroid photo of myself wearing a dated flowered print dress.

I knew this wedding day was nearly twenty years old: Ouch! Within seconds a flood of memories came back about this charming, no-frills wedding I had coordinated years before in the backyard of a bride and groom's rocky hillside fixer-upper home above Los Angeles.

The property was nestled in and around a grove of scrub oak trees. The road up to the home was dusty and filled with gravel-sized clots of clay weathered by drought and hardened into a passable roadbed by four-wheel drive vehicles.

Except for the cake delivery the wedding day set up was completed in good time. I was anxious for the cake to arrive so we could start the ceremony without being interrupted by the sound of the delivery vehicle's engine working its way up the steep driveway.

The cake was the one professional culinary splurge our bride Sandra set her heart on. She and her favorite Aunt Tara had prepared most of the main dishes a couple of days before the wedding. The guests were asked to bring side dishes and appetizers as their wedding presents. Sandra was really looking forward to her elaborate three-layer stacked cake edged in a lace pattern that mimicked her delicate gown.

With its intricate fondant lace applique trimming, no one among Sandra's family or friends wanted to attempt to decorate the wedding cake. I warned the bakery to take it easy driving up the hill to deliver the cake and to make sure the driver left ample time due to the roughness of the road.

On the day of the wedding after most of the guests were seated, I telephoned the bakery to get an accurate time of arrival. The manager said the driver had left in plenty of time, so hopefully the cake would arrive any moment. The classical string trio continued to play. As the afternoon sun moved across the property, the musicians needed to adjust their position under the old oak tree to protect their instruments from the harsh August sun.

Another five minutes passed and the groom, Dennis, began pacing nervously, unseen by Sandra who was waiting on her second-story perch for my signal to walk down the exterior wooden staircase for her entrance in the processional.

I didn't blame him. Even though the sun was still high in the sky, we didn't have any ancillary lighting to help after sundown. Dennis knew that the setting sun would signal the end of the reception. The tiny staff we hired for the day had already been informed that this might be a flashlight tear-down.

There just wasn't any money in the budget for lighting or even an assistant to help me pass out programs, move guests, receive side dishes, and perform sign-in duties. I was a few hours ahead of schedule setting up tables and chairs, then putting down linen and silverware to ease the labor hours of the one server and bartender hired for the reception.

Even though I knew from the start that this wedding was going to be labor intensive for me and, quite frankly, a scramble on the wedding day, I really liked Sandra and Dennis and wanted to be a part of their wedding team. I admired how much work they had done on their house since I first met them several months previously. They had transformed an ordinary tract house into a charming home, doing most of the work themselves.

Fortunately, Aunt Tara stepped in again and became my lookout while I gave the musicians the cue to begin the processional. With her mind totally focused on the ceremony, Sandra never once asked me about the cake or any other detail, and I was thrilled she was living in the moment. One way or another we would have a cake, even if I had to go to a market following the ceremony, purchase a few cake layers, and build a tiered wedding cake myself.

I had arranged for a skeleton catering crew consisting of one bartender, one server for the buffet, and one scullery staff person to help clear tables and wash any serving pieces and silverware for the 75 guests. Sandra even thought to ask her guests to bring their side dishes in throw-away foil trays to avoid the trouble of washing lots of pots and pans.

Sandra and Dennis provided the main dishes themselves and with guests having brought the side dishes, and the bartender providing all the beverages, I was able to concentrate on organizing the layout of the buffet. After the ceremony the bartender set up the table bar while the guests watched the photo shoot and munched on fresh vegetables, cheeses, cold cuts, and dips from a self-serve display.

Since renting big market umbrellas was not in the budget, Sandra and Dennis found affordable individual white paper umbrellas that shielded their guests from the hot rays of the late summer day. Guests availed themselves of any shade they could find under the same old oak tree the musicians had cornered earlier for the ceremony.

Sandra's Aunt Tara had volunteered to stay in front of the house to wait for the cake van while I styled the buffet dishes. Finally, just as the bride and groom were finishing the post-ceremony photo shoot, the cake arrived. I relieved Aunt Tara so she could join the other guests while I assisted the delivery person up the stairs with the cake. Mission finally accomplished.

The rest of the afternoon went just as we all planned. As dusk fell over the back yard, it was time to cut the cake. I felt like the Pied Piper as all the guests followed me up the deck stairs into the large screened porch and dining room space while Sandra and Dennis used the front entrance to get back into the house to freshen up a bit before rejoining us.

Sandra and Dennis wanted to take part in the time-honored rituals of saying a few words of thanks to their guests, then cutting and feeding each other a piece of cake, and finally sampling the culinary smorgasbord.

Dennis gently served a fork full of cake to Sandra who returned the favor, but with a visible wince as the taste of the cake settled in her own mouth. She asked me for two glasses of water stat, and I dashed to the kitchen. Once they both took a few gulps, Sandra whispered that I should taste the cake before she turned back to her guests and asked them to follow her and Dennis downstairs to the backyard for coffee, cake, and dancing before nightfall.

I knew something had gone horribly wrong with the cake as soon as Sandra subverted our original plan to serve it immediately while the guests were still upstairs. Without a full staff of servers, the cake couldn't be served to the tables downstairs in a timely fashion.

I sampled a forkful from each of the three layers and with each bite the extreme saltiness told me the bakery must have miss measured the amount salt. The taste of salt was so overpowering that I could have mixed it with water and gargled with it. There was no quick fix for this bakery boo-boo.

Literally from out of nowhere, Aunt Tara came over to me and said she was watching to learn how to cut a multilayered cake and noticed we had abandoned the wedding cake. Was something wrong, she asked?

Normally, I wouldn't have shared a cake disaster with a guest but Aunt Tara's friendly, concerned attitude relaxed my defenses. I told her the sad story and she was right there with a solution. She explained that she had petit fours in containers that were to be used for tomorrow's brunch. She had also brought lots of fresh fruit to share while everyone was getting ready, but no one had touched it.

"Let's just serve the pastries and fruit instead of the cake," she offered, again becoming my instant assistant coordinator. Together, we arranged several attractive trays of petite fours and fruit and delivered them to the buffet table, which the server had cleared during the cake cutting ceremony.

Helping me figure out a quick fix for the cake fiasco wasn't Aunt Tara's only contribution to the success of the wedding day. She was the first person on the scene and got the bride off to a great start by helping with her hair and makeup and then assisting her with her gown, giving me time to talk to the services as they arrived at the property to set up.

All day she was Johnny-on-the-spot wherever she was needed. Aunt Tara greeted guests when Dennis's cousins weren't on time to receive side dishes. Then she manned the receiving table, handing out programs and paper umbrellas while I was making sure the immediate family members were all together for the last few photos before the ceremony, out of view of our arriving guests.

In short, I couldn't have done this wedding without her assistance. From that day on, I knew I could no longer do a wedding without at least one assistant. Aunt Tara was my unexpected guardian angel and wedding day assistant. I will always be grateful.

I continue to be blessed by wonderful assistants now numbering as high as four or five when a wedding calls for it. They work diligently, making sure everything is set up for the ceremony, cocktail, and reception areas and acting as my eyes and ears in the front of the house while I'm attending to the family, bridesmaids and of course our bride during prep time.

There is no substitute for great teamwork. Once the bride and groom, if they are seeing each other before the ceremony, begin taking photos and video coverage, I am able to review the various set-ups across the property, confer with services, greet family and gather wedding party members for photos as needed. Having that personal touch is so important on the wedding day. Just as Aunt Tara did instinctively years ago, my assistants today sense what is needed and adjust to the circumstances, coming up with solutions and moving on to the next task at hand.

Chapter 10

Unsung Wedding Heroes

As with Aunt Tara, the real unsung heroes are those individuals who are not on your payroll, but just step in when needed, without any expectations, and often times just in the nick of time to salvage a crumbling cake or out of control toddlers bent on getting their needs met just as their mother walks down the aisle as the matron of honor.

One such potential disaster was avoided thanks to one such friend and colleague's quick thinking and road racing skills, the nimble fingers of a seamstress, and an alert assistant who helped me save my reputation, and make one foreign bride's first American experience truly joyful.

I felt really fortunate to be hired for this charming small wedding that joined Michael with Yumi, his Japanese bride still living in Japan. The few Japanese words I had learned when I was in Japan on unrelated business trips a decade earlier really came in handy. The bride and groom had already been married in Japan, but Michael's family and friends lived in the United States, so it was great that Michael and his bride, Yumi, could come back to the U.S. briefly for another ceremony for his side of the family. Joyce (her American name), the sister of the groom, lived in Los Angeles and contacted me to help her organize her brother's wedding just a few months away.

After speaking with Joyce, she put me in touch with her parents who would be hosting the wedding but lived in Montana on a ranch. While

Joyce's mother said that this wedding would be small, she stressed that both the flowers and her daughter-in-law's dress be beautiful for photos. Yumi planned to arrive a week before the wedding with her groom, Michael. We would need a few days to make sure the dress her mother-in-law found for Yumi in the United States would be fitted properly considering she would be nearly five months pregnant by the wedding date, only three months away.

They weren't planning to start a family so quickly after they got married, but nature had taken center stage, leaving us to move as fast as we could to set up the wedding. We had to pick a sample dress in stock due to the short lead time. It was a guessing game as to what size to order so I suggested an empire A-line design with pleats in the back and front that could be let out if we needed to open up the width of the dress to make more room. There was no manufacturer at the time with this specific design, so we found a wedding gown shop that would take two dresses and use the bodice of one dress and the skirt of another.

Since Yumi only spoke Japanese and my vocabulary was so meager, it was best to have Joyce interpret for me what Yumi had in mind for flowers during our only conversation, a three-way live chat over the phone. Yumi wanted two large bouquets for the altar area and mini bouquets just for Michael's mother, and sister-in-law, Joyce. A simple but elegant bouquet of pink peonies for Yumi and a single peony for Michael was also requested. The fathers along with the best man would wear light pink roses.

The centerpieces for the dinner table would be a series of vases, lush blossoms and crystal candlesticks going down the center of an eighteen-foot rectangular table set for nine guests on either side. Votive lights with small bouquets of roses and peonies would cluster at the base of the crystal candlesticks. Yumi wanted a romantic-looking table styled to allow guests on opposite sides to see each other between candlesticks.

We dispensed with the ceremony rehearsal to give Yumi and her groom Michael some extra time to relax before the immediate family started to arrive in town a day or two before the wedding. Yumi reported that her final fitting went very well on Wednesday before the wedding and the dress was pressed and ready for pick up by Friday morning.

For their ceremony Yumi and Michael selected a small chapel overlooking the Pacific Ocean in Malibu. Dinner would follow at a boutique hotel in Beverly Hills where many family members had booked rooms for the wedding week.

I had made my final follow-up calls to all the wedding services and we were good to go. Saturday came and Yumi arrived with her sister-in-law, Joyce, acting as her maid of honor.

Joyce and I began helping Yumi into her dress when we realized that between Wednesday and Saturday afternoon the baby must have shifted and the dress was now too snug and wouldn't zip up. Normally I can sew well enough to make adjustments, but this dress really needed a professional touch, given that it had already been adjusted once, leaving very little extra seam allowance in critical areas.

I called the gown shop to see if they could give me any instructions as to how the alterations could be made. To my surprise and delight, the store owner said one of her seamstresses lives only minutes away from our chapel and she would call her and have her come over herself to fix the dress, even though it was her day off, at no charge. Sure enough, in fifteen minutes Gloria showed up and saved the day.

By the time Gloria arrived it was time for me to check on the flowers. Before I could reach the chapel from the changing rooms in an adjoining building, I got a call from my assistant Laurie who was at the hotel helping set up the dinner reception area. Laurie told me that the florist's assistant had just dropped off the reception flowers. Immediately I knew that was a problem because the plans had called for the florist to first deliver the flowers to the chapel and then to the hotel. We really needed to have the personal flowers on hand twenty minutes before we had planned to start our photos. Somehow the florist had gotten the delivery times switched and went to the hotel first. With the assistant florist at the hotel we could only hope that the head florist was en route to the chapel and would be there shortly.

I called the florist shop and the cell number, but no answer. Our ceremony was an hour and a half away and we simply had to get those flowers in time for the ceremony, if not the photo session. I had this awful feeling in the pit of my stomach that something was wrong and perhaps the florist went to the wrong church. I started calling all the churches in the area to see if any florist had shown up with flowers meant for our wedding. No missing flowers at the other churches. Where could the florist be? The florist was now at least forty-five minutes late and we were less than an hour from our ceremony time.

I called the one grocery store in the area to see if they had any flowers that we could buy to make a bouquet and boutonnieres as a last resort. Unfortunately, no flowers in our color palette were in stock. In desperation I called a florist friend, Luis, who was about 35 minutes away, and asked him if he had any flowers of the right colors that he could bring to the chapel. He was able to gather some pale peach and some small pale pink roses. With his assistant assembling the bouquets and boutonnieres in the back of the truck, Luis drove through the winding canyon road to the chapel. He arrived ten minutes ahead of the ceremony start time. I still don't know how he made it to the chapel so quickly, although still too late for pre-wedding photos.

Even though the ceremony proceeded with only personal flowers, the parents of the groom were so gracious and just wanted to know if we could take photos after the ceremony if the correct flowers arrived by then. I assured them we would do everything we could to make sure the photos would be taken with the proper flowers.

I secretly prayed that the original flowers would suddenly appear and about ten minutes into the ceremony my prayers were answered. The flowers finally arrived in two pairs of hands, both sweating nervously. I literally looked up to the heavens and said thank you Lord.

I didn't know if I should admonish the florist for being so late or hug him for finally getting there with the flowers in one piece. I took one look at him and his helper and knew that something really difficult had happened.

He apologized for the delivery mix up explaining that a traffic accident in a tunnel had them stuck for nearly forty minutes, compounding the problem. I decided it was not the time to talk about the blunder of going to the hotel first and just asked the florist to wait until the ceremony was over to place the large bouquets and stands inside the chapel for post-ceremony photos. He obliged happily.

Luis, my guardian angel florist didn't ask for payment, but I made sure that the original florist reimbursed him for his time and materials. The original florist understood how he had disappointed the bride and her mother-in-law and didn't charge my client for the ceremony and personal flowers either. After the ceremony members of the wedding party exchanged their make-do flowers for the original ones and gathered for photos. Then they went on to the hotel for a wonderful dinner. God may have intervened, but my faithful friend Luis and colleague Gloria saved the day.

More Wedding Heroes to Mention:

As a wedding planner I have been the recipient of so many acts of kindness and generosity that my faith in people is renewed again and again. I offer my heartfelt thanks to the many unnamed people who stepped in at a moment's notice to save the day. If any of them should read these words they will know again just how appreciated they are for making someone else's wedding day dreams come true.

Thank you to the server who caught my faulty skirt zipper and held my skirt waistband as I was making my way over to the bride and groom's table to deliver their champagne flutes for a toast.

Thank you to the server who ran up six flights of stairs to make sure a diabetic grandma had dinner on time when the elevator wasn't working.

Thank you to the catering manager who recognized that there was a mistake in the spelling of the bride's name on the printed menus that arrived before I was on property and found a printing company to print, cut, and deliver new ones in time for my crew to place them inside the napkins.

Thank you to the catering manager who upon finding out that the owner of the property was planning on removing all the antique furniture from the lobby and the cocktail areas, saved some pieces for us for our wedding day. The caterer returned the pieces to the owner immediately the next day following the wedding day.

Thank you to the photographer who covered for me while I went back to my home office to retrieve my event notebook which I had left next to the garage door when packing up the car earlier in the morning.

Gratefully, I had arrived very early to the site and the client hadn't expected my arrival until I had returned for the second time.

Thank you to the numerous servers who have offered to get drinks for the bride and groom only to return with "weak" drinks that would assure that the happy couple didn't consume too much alcohol in all the excitement.

Thank you to the florist who supplied a complimentary roll of tulle to a bride when her veiling went missing from her room hours before the wedding.

Thank you to the band leader who jumped down from the stage and began singing and playing his guitar on the dance floor surrounded by the guests when the electricity went out for twenty minutes and saved the momentum of the evening.

Thank you to all the valets who stepped in and helped move tables and chairs, set linen, and table top items while the ceremony was going on to cover for members of the catering crew who didn't show because of illness.

Thank you to the many family members of bridal couples that generously stepped in behind the scenes to clean up messes and take wedding gifts home at the end of the evening when a best man or maid of honor had enjoyed themselves a bit too much.

Thank you to the photographer that noticed a guest was getting in my face toward the end of the event and came to my side before the guest created a scene.

Hopefully in future writings I will be able to share the stories of so many more individuals who have made the effort to do what was needed without reward or recognition.

Chapter 11

The Artist's Way:

When I first saw my husband several years before we actually got to know each other, I formed an opinion by observing him during weddings. I remember thinking he was a very good-looking man, talented musician, and seemed to have an easygoing nature. He was always polite to me when we passed in a hallway. He seemed to have fun on stage, yet he was very focused and in the moment when he was performing as a singer/trumpet player.

It wasn't until we started dating that I became more aware of his artist's temperament. I thought I understood what an artist's viewpoint and behaviors were like. After all, there were artists in my family and at one point I thought of myself as a budding artist and still dream of creating works of art today.

I know what it is like to get lost in a project, losing my sense of time because I am so immersed in the creative process. However, I can easily slip out of that groove when responsibility calls; not so much for Bill.

Once I became an art teacher, I kept on creating in a sense, but I was focused first on my students so my job became to nurture worthwhile, creative experiences for them. Later in my career when I designed products for the gift and housewares industry, I created products based on what would sell or fit the market at hand, not on what pleased me personally.

Even as a wedding planner, I tried to fill the creative needs of others with suggestions and concepts to make their wedding visions come alive…all worthwhile endeavors and I am so grateful for the opportunity to have been in and around so many creative minds in the process.

What I have witnessed in my husband and so many of my clients and creative wedding services is their allegiance to an inner artistic drive and voice to express themselves in their own unique way. Time is a relative factor in many cases during the process. Artists take the time they need to accomplish a task, goal, or commitment. They are not generally nine-to-fivers.

Sometimes ideas or decisions take time to percolate or simmer, until the final distillation of what is desired culminates in a final decision. Recently, I read an excerpt from "A Swingin' Show-biz Saga," a memoir by Paul Shaffer, the musical director for the David Letterman Show. In his book Shaffer writes about how he tried for weeks to get Sammy Davis Jr. to return a call about a music number for an upcoming show. Paul needed to know what song Sammy wanted to sing and in what key he wanted to sing it, so he could present the band with an arrangement of the song that would work best for Sammy.

On the morning of the show Paul was finally able to confirm the tune and key, leaving him only a few hours to write an arrangement and rehearse it with the band.

Sammy arrived at the television studio about an hour before the show began taping and Paul pressed him to take a few minutes to listen to a tape of the arrangement to make sure Sammy would like it and be able to sing it comfortably. Sammy just remarked that he knew the song and not to bother having him listen to it, but Paul was concerned that Sammy may not like his arrangement and it would show in the performance. With Paul's insistence, Sammy relented and sat down and listened to the tape.

This little episode reminded me of one of my brides who was a professional ballerina. After working with her for a few months she told me in the nicest terms that I was overwhelming her with too many documents and requests for decisions.

The other wedding services were waiting anxiously as well for final decisions and in some cases signed agreements. She kindly told me she was a last-minute kind of gal and everything always works out just fine. Was she channeling how Sammy Davis Jr. felt all those years ago?

I took a deep breath and realized that my dedication to creating a perfect wedding day for my client was overshadowing the creative process she required. If I had known initially that this bride was a last-minute decision maker, I would have steered her toward a higher level of coordination services which would have given her more flexibility, while providing me with more support from an office assistant who would handle last-minute details and communications if I was busy working on another upcoming event.

Much like Paul Shaffer, I just wanted to get everything right for the client. After coordinating countless weddings and working with so many different personalities I knew that expecting someone to change their behavior for a specific event in their life just doesn't happen.

An added problem in situations like these is that not everyone reveals all aspects of their personality immediately. I found out that when it comes to his work, Bill is intensely focused and when those earphones are on and he is at his computer working on music copying and arranging, it's best to leave him alone until he comes up for air. All Sammy wanted when he got to the studio was to rest and recharge himself for the evening.

It's easy to make the assumption that if you present someone with three choices and they know you have done the background work, all they should have to do is say yea or nay. People like Paul Shaffer and myself just need an answer or at least reassurance that we are on the right track.

In the case of Sammy Davis Jr., he just wanted to live in the moment. He was confident in his ability to make the song work whether the arrangement was great or not. Paul was the one that was in a rush, being concerned about the quality of his work as I was with my ballerina bride.

Too often I have found myself rushing to do something when, in reality, we are better off feeling the moment and acting on our instincts. For more than twenty-five years now I've been keeping time, keeping pace, and keeping on keeping on. Now that I've stepped off the wedding planner express and boarded another train traveling in a different direction toward a destination not yet fully known, something tells me it's time to stop and enjoy each moment as it passes for as long as possible.

I hope I have found my voice in this book and you will listen to it and find something of merit in the road stories that follow.

Section 2

Road Stories (Weddings and Lessons Learned)

Chapter 1

When Real Life Interrupts the Wedding Plans:

When you really love someone, it's hard to be separated, even if only for short distances and spans of time, let alone endure a separation of eight thousand miles under uncertain circumstances. Sure, today you can phone, text and Skype to feel connected with your loved one, but not long ago, overseas phone calls were expensive and difficult to place, especially to the Ukraine which, in the late 1980s when this wedding took place, was part of the Soviet Union. Such was the case for one of my first clients, Allison and Robert, as they struggled to find a way to get married, living so far apart.

When I met Allison, the bride, she described herself as an English teacher living in New England and her fiancé, Robert, as a gifted writer. They had met in England on scholarships three years prior to their engagement. At that time, Allison, an American, was doing her junior year abroad studying English while Robert had left his native land, the Soviet Union, to take advantage of a prestigious year-long graduate scholarship.

These two strangers met in a chance encounter as they agreed to share a cab on a rainy day in London. I know, this sounds like a scene from a movie and well, it might as well have been a movie; the effort it took for Allison and Robert to get married amounted to a cinematic feat of courage and character.

Once Allison and Robert returned to their respective countries, they carried on a long distance relationship through letters and infrequent phone calls for nearly three years. There were times when Allison and Robert had scheduled phone calls, but at the appointed time Robert was mysteriously unavailable.

I only became privy to these difficulties when Allison failed to follow through on some topics I asked her to discuss with Robert in preparation for their wedding ceremony. Allison would leave a cryptic phone message letting me know Robert wasn't available for the planned talk so she couldn't answer my questions.

This wedding occurred early in my wedding planner career and I was not yet well schooled in the emotional roller coaster some brides and grooms experience. I just felt there was more to the story than Allison was sharing with me. She seemed very moody at times and even terse when I spoke with her over the phone.

I was hired by the temple to conduct a meeting with the wedding couple in order to settle their selection of a florist, photographer, videographer, and other services, and to make final follow-up calls to establish a schedule of load-in and load-out at the temple. I was responsible for cueing each event: the wedding services for the ceremony, the bride as to when she should be dressing, and the photographer and families to begin pre-ceremony photography.

Since several caterers had working privileges at the temple, I would find out which one the bride and groom had selected and notify them as to when the ceremony would conclude and food service begin, cue the kitchen to serve the first course once the guests in the ballroom had concluded the hora (traditional Hebrew circle dance), speeches, and motzi (blessing over the challah bread).

Another factor that was causing some anxiety was the fact that the temple was brand new and was still in the final stages of construction. Allison didn't seem at all interested in the timing of events or even discussing what the flowers were supposed to look like. She kept focusing on whether mezuzahs had been placed on the door jams of all the rooms in the Synagogue. Now I understood the significance of the mezuzahs, a symbol of God's blessing over the house of worship, and the necessity to have them mounted on the newly constructed Temple doors before the wedding day, but Allison was so fixated on this one thing that I began to question if something else wasn't afoot. I began to think maybe it was me and she would be better off working with someone else. I just felt she didn't want to talk to me about the ceremony at all.

The wedding only a month away, I went to the administration building at the Temple to ask about the mezuzahs. I thought if I can get one thing off Allison's plate, hopefully she would be calmer, happier and more receptive to talking about the wedding. The secretary asked me to take a seat and she would get someone to answer my question. After waiting a few minutes, Rabbi Simon came into the office.

"So glad to see you again," he said, extending his hand in a firm and friendly greeting. I was so surprised to be greeted by the rabbi since I expected to be talking to the building manager about the mezuzahs.

"So you have met Allison already?" he asked.

I explained that I had met her and she seemed very concerned that I make sure all the rooms that they will be using for their wedding have been blessed with a mezuzah mounted in the door jam.

The rabbi responded that technically some final details to the building had to be finished before they could have the ceremony of placing mezuzahs on the door jams. Then I decided to confide my fears. I told him that Allison just didn't seem happy talking to me and I was wondering if I was just not the right person to help her.

Rabbi Simon smiled and interrupted me. "It's not you, Tobey. There's a lot more to the story." He went on to explain that Robert lived in the Ukraine and was considered a Refusnik, an activist in the U.S.S.R. who was denied the opportunity to emigrate to Israel where he could practice his religion openly, something that was forbidden at the time in the Soviet Union.

Robert, in fact, had become very influential in the Refusnik movement in the last few years and was recognized as one of its leaders.

"As we speak," Rabbi Simon went on to say, "he is attempting to arrange to get out of the U.S.S.R., but there is a warrant out for his arrest. He has to find a way out secretly. If the press learns of his intent to leave, it's bad news for him and Allison. Our conversation today is confidential as you must understand." I nodded silently.

In the recent past, Robert had been detained and interrogated by the Soviet police and was on a list of possible enemies of the state…pretty heavy stuff for sure. The Rabbi told me that no one else at the temple knew of the situation but himself and now me.

I told the Rabbi that I had heard of this movement in the Soviet Union but had no idea how serious it was or that Robert's life might be in danger if the authorities got wind that he was trying to leave his homeland and resettle elsewhere. Allison literally didn't know if Robert would make it out of the Soviet Union and to the United States by the wedding date.

To protect the couple, the name "Robert" had been adopted as Alison's fiancé's code name. To avoid detection if mail was intercepted, Allison wrote to the equivalent of a post office box address, as she didn't know exactly where Robert was living at the time.

After the Rabbi's briefing I developed a newfound respect for Allison and the stress she must have been feeling as her fiancé managed a high-stakes international political escape. Would he make it out of the Soviet Union safely and then find transport to the United States and on to California in time for their wedding?

Even though Allison and Robert were both Jewish, Allison was a conservative congregate and the new temple was the same. Robert was a very devout Jew who practiced orthodoxy and lived by a strict code of religious practices.

At the time, according to Jewish law, an Orthodox marriage could not take place inside a conservative temple sanctuary, but the ceremony could take place outside on the grounds of the temple. Security was added for the wedding day because it was possible that the news of Robert's arrival in the United States might be publicized, bringing on a flurry of news trucks, cameras, and commotion.

As the wedding day approached Allison was both excited and nervous beyond belief. She knew that her life was about to change drastically. She would be living as an orthodox married lady, wearing a wig to cover her real hair in public. She would soon follow all the dietary laws and would no longer shake men's hands, nor would she wear pants or show her legs in public. She knew that her relationship with her parents and siblings would change as well since they would not share her Orthodox religious practices.

She didn't even know when she would see them again if she had to follow Robert out of the U.S. to continue his quest to get as many Jews out of the Soviet Union to other countries using undercover methods. Would Robert be granted political asylum or be protected in some way that would allow him to keep on traveling and helping others? No one knew for sure. That was a lot for Allison to process.

Two days ahead of the wedding I learned that Allison got word that Robert was on route to the United States. Technically a wanted man in the Soviet Union, Robert had somehow made it through customs and on to California the night before the wedding.

On the wedding day Allison would see her groom when he arrived at the temple just minutes before the ceremony. When I received word that Robert was less than an hour away I gently knocked on the door to the bride's room to give Allison the good news. Hearing nothing, I opened the door a crack to see Allison sitting in her bathrobe at the bride's table in front of the large mirror, her head hanging down and arms out-stretched grasping the ends of the table like she was in deep thought or meditation. I closed the door to give her some more time. I came back in about ten minutes hoping she would acknowledge me so I could let her know it was time to get dressed.

Again I gently knocked on the door and took one step into the room. She said, "I need to be alone. " I said, "Certainly. I just wanted you to know Robert is expected here in less than an hour and if you need any help getting into your dress, I would be happy to help you."

"Not now," Allison said firmly, and I quickly closed the door and left her alone. I took a deep breath trying to compose myself. I felt like I had just been slapped in the face verbally and hoped I hadn't offended her.

When Allison's mother approached me in the hall outside the changing room, she asked me if Allison was dressed. I told her that she wanted to be alone and she would let us know when she needed help dressing. Allison's mother nodded and said she'd check on her daughter in a few minutes to which I responded that I would be outside checking on the arrival of the guests and to let me know if her daughter needed anything.

Suddenly the details of who walks with whom and in what order didn't seem important. The sound system was finally operational and was working outside for the first time. Somehow we were going to have a wedding that day and it really didn't matter whether it would be in picture perfect order or not.

I gathered the Kiddush cup and the glass to break and placed them on a small wooden table where the Chuppah (tallit cover connected to four poles) would be standing, held up by four men. Outside I heard a group of footsteps climbing the concrete stairs from the parking lot leading to the outdoor courtyard. Robert had arrived with his entourage.

Robert and the rest of the Jewish males joined together for a brief ceremony to review the Ketubah (Jewish Marriage contract) before joining the women to veil (Bedecken) Allison and sign the Ketubah.

The pre ceremony traditions completed, with his best man and two other Rabbis, Robert walked proudly down the aisle as Allison, just inside the glass temple doors, stood between her parents clutching her bouquet and small white bible she had received on her Bat Mitzvah years before.

Her mother carefully brought her blusher forward to shield her face. It rested just below her lace covered, long-sleeved ivory gown. The catering manager and I opened the doors and Allison emerged taking one step at a time down the few shallow stairs to the courtyard flanked by her parents to the traditional Hebrew melody, Do Di Le.

At the conclusion of the wedding ceremony I stored the Kiddush cup they drank from and the glass Robert had broken as keepsakes and the simple Chuppah cover made from a large tallit (Jewish prayer shawl). The cloth top and four wooden poles were returned to the small chapel adjacent to the courtyard for safekeeping.

I kept thinking that Robert having made it safely to the United States was a triumph in itself. He could have been intercepted and returned to the Soviet Union to face the iron arm of discrimination and cruelty by being incarcerated for many years.

The Sunday afternoon sky above was a bright blue hue interrupted only by the occasional white streak of a passing cloud. I hoped the sky would prove to be an apt metaphor for Allison and Robert's future together.

Chapter 2

The Groom who held a Wedding Hostage to his Hidden Fears.

I recognize that men and women think differently and therefore react differently to situations. But when I stand witness to the early skirmishes of a simmering wedding war between the bride's mother and the groom, I pray that calmer minds will prevail.

This wedding was not the Hatfields and McCoys, but rather a pitch battle about the value of a dollar and how it should be spent, even if the person voicing the most dire concerns wasn't paying the tab. There are no villains here, just hard-working, decent people whose agendas had been nurtured and cured by their own life experiences and family values.

The flash point came at our first budget meeting where I wanted to get a feel as to whether the priorities and tastes of Carolyn and Robert (our bride and groom) were compatible with the standards and budget constraints of Carolyn's parents, Angela and Harry.

Prior to this initial meeting, Carolyn and Robert had already discussed what they wanted for the wedding day, so Robert didn't join us. Frankly, it's not uncommon for the groom to sit out the early meetings and join in later once the big topic of budget has been handled, especially when the parents of the bride are footing the bill for the entire wedding.

Even Harry sat out the first two hours when Carolyn, Angela and I discussed the elements that would determine the "look" of the wedding from the style of Carolyn's wedding dress to the flowers and tabletop set-ups. As we reviewed magazine tear sheets and scrolled through dozens of Pinterest pages, Carolyn's desires melded nicely with her mother's fine taste and sensibilities, allowing a beautiful cohesive wedding day design to emerge. Once we completed the "look" of the wedding, we went on to talk about the wedding party and family members to plan what roles they would each play in the pre-wedding day activities and on the wedding day itself.

Again, I was pleased to find that mom and daughter were pretty much on the same page. Angela and Carolyn spirited each other on, making the most of their compatibility and yet being respectful of each other when occasional differences in taste and style arose.

When the focus of the discussion turned to how the desired wedding was going to fit into the pre-established $60,000 budget, Harry suddenly appeared as if he had been waiting at the door for his cue. He suggested we move from the dining room table into the living room where he sat in a wing-backed chair next to the fireplace while Carolyn and her mother nestled in among the soft down pillows on the comfy couch facing the fireplace. I sat down across from Harry in a club chair that swiveled so I could turn easily from mother and daughter to the father of the bride. No doubt, we ladies were a bit giddy with pride in what we had accomplished during our two-hour design and style conference over the dining room table.

Angela had set a tray of coffee and some terrific homemade scones on the coffee table for us to refuel while I gave Harry an overview of what had been discussed before he joined us. We were munching on the scones when Harry decided it was time to unleash his tirade about responsible financial planning. The room turned cold when he turned to his wife and said in a serious tone, "Now, we do have an understanding that this wedding isn't going over $60,000, no matter what happens!" Stone-faced, Angela, Carolyn, and I all nodded obediently.

Harry unloaded his impassioned arsenal of whys, wherefores, and how comes regarding this firm financial ceiling, speaking not only for his family's sake but for my benefit as well to avoid any potential misunderstandings. I got the message loud and clear.

A few weeks later with firmer estimates on the reception costs, Robert joined us for the second meeting where we discussed the flow of the wedding day plus the music, photography, food likes and dislikes. I was trying to get a handle on the categories in which I was told Robert wanted input. There were no shortage of opinions when it came to choosing the bar and dance songs, as well as how to make sure the photographer wasn't in the couple's faces too much during the wedding day.

Robert was respectful when addressing me, but he followed my every statement with a chorus of "How come?" "Is that normal?" "Does it have to be that way?" I wasn't sure if he was just an extremely curious person or if he really didn't like his fiancée's taste. Maybe he felt it was easier to lash out at me rather than start an argument with his intended.

Carolyn didn't say anything to her mom or me about Robert's behavior at the meeting until a few days later when the three of us were on a conference call to discuss setting up appointments to interview photographers. Then she mentioned that Robert wasn't happy with the cost of her dress. Angela asked somewhat indignantly why he had to know what they were spending on anything. Who knew that Robert could turn what had seemed to be a straightforward process of planning and paying for a wedding into an attempted kidnapping of hopes and dreams?

From Angela's perspective, as soon as the couple became engaged, her future son-in-law — who she thought was so perfect for her daughter — had suddenly morphed into an alien bean counter, frantically challenging the cost of each item in a wedding to which he was contributing not one cent.

Angela mentioned that Robert's inquiries felt like a Gatling gun spewing out question after question in rapid succession: Why did we need up lights? What's the point of spending money on lace overlays? "For God's sake," the mother of the bride said. "What's it to him? He isn't paying for the wedding. We don't have a mortgage anymore; he does. No one asked him to pay for anything. What is his beef really about?"

In my heart, I knew that Angela and Carolyn weren't cooking up some outrageous scheme for an over-the-top wedding in which crystal chandeliers brought in from Austria would hang over the guests' heads during the cocktail hour while trained exotic animals roamed freely on falcate rugs.

Angela hated to see her daughter stressed about any wedding detail. This was supposed to be a wonderful sharing time for Angela and her daughter. Carolyn so wanted to find a way to explain to Robert that the wedding wasn't going to be over the top; it would be a tasteful, quality wedding for 160 guests.

Carolyn and her mom had a really close relationship and wouldn't think of keeping anything from each other. It wasn't like they were in each other's business; rather, if something was weighing heavily on either of their minds or hearts they had a safe place to express it and work together if needed to solve the problem or work around the obstacle.

But this conversation wasn't the normal mother/daughter pow-wow. This situation involved Carolyn's most cherished relationships: The man she wanted to spend the rest of her life with and her mother who just wanted her to have the wedding of her dreams.

I heard the strain in Carolyn's voice as she struggled to repeat Robert's words; that he would have a really hard time knowing that the family couldn't figure out a way to spend significantly less than $60,000 on a wedding. To Robert, it was the principal of not dropping a huge amount of money on a single day of their lives. To his credit, Robert had put himself through pharmacology school, paid back his student loans within five years, and purchased a condo for Carolyn and himself to move into before the wedding to set up housekeeping.

Not wanting to ignore her fiancé's concerns, Carolyn felt that maybe there was more to the issue than he was expressing. She called me after another round of cost debates wondering if there was a solution to Robert's anxiety about the wedding budget.

I donned my psychologist's hat and asked her what kind of childhood Robert had with his parents and siblings. Were they comfortable financially or did they have to watch their pennies? The more I found out about Robert and his family the more I understood where he was coming from. His grandfather, to whom he was very close while growing up, suffered through very hard times on a farm in the Midwest during the Great Depression. Life was rough and Robert's grandfather saw his parents stretch every dollar as far as it could go to provide for the entire family. His grandfather's values were handed down and practiced, even though Robert's parents had secure jobs with pensions. They were helping to support Robert's grandmother, which put a real strain on their future retirement resources. His family history explained much of his attitude toward spending for the wedding, but in my mind it still didn't account for such a strong reaction.

Carolyn mentioned how fortunate she was to have parents who invested early in their married life and could afford to give her such a lovely wedding. Her parents weren't the type to flaunt their prosperity, but they enjoyed indulging on special vacations and Carolyn's mom had a killer shoe collection in her closet, a situation of which Robert was aware.

Carolyn's standard of living growing up was quite a bit higher than Robert's. Perhaps at the bottom of all the fuss was his fear that he would not be able to support Carolyn in the manner in which she had been accustomed, and therefore, if he didn't watch spending now with Carolyn, they might have a hard time managing in years to come.

Since Robert was a serious-minded fellow, I couldn't help thinking that he might be projecting into the future to a day when a daughter of his own would get married. Would he be able to provide her with the kind of wedding Carolyn and he were about to experience?

I encouraged Carolyn to try to create a safe way for Robert to express his fears about spending and see if his anxiety about money didn't come down to a fear of disappointing her and their future family someday. Sure enough, to Carolyn's credit, she did talk to Robert and together they recognized his concern about measuring up to the standard of living Carolyn's father had established for his family.

Once all the uncomfortable feelings were released, Robert and Carolyn together settled on a set of family values and how they would practice them moving forward in marriage and making a life together.

It's hard to talk about everything before you get married, but I learned through my own pre-marital counseling with Bill just how important it is that your value systems align when it comes to money, religion, and raising a family together.

Bill and I sat across from a family counselor a few months before our wedding wanting to make sure we got off to a good start. Barbara, our counselor, had helped me traverse the emotional mountainous trail of divorce and uncertainty nearly twelve years earlier, so I knew she would give us both wonderful insight into how to approach many issues that were bound to come up blending two families, handling money, religious and cultural differences before our wedding day.

When it came to talking about money, we both kind of froze. Suddenly the room became very quiet and I wasn't sure if it would help or harm if I started to share my concerns. Bill, being a musician, music copyist and vocal arranger was used to riding a feast-or-famine financial roller coaster. Neither of us had nine-to-five jobs as a roadmap to stay the course. I knew that Bill had amassed some debt over the years and I wanted to avoid carrying debt into our marriage. In front of Barbara I asked him how he would want to handle that. He quickly whipped out his wallet and handed it to me. We all had a chuckle and I said, "Does this mean you want me to be in charge of paying the bills?" He smiled broadly and I swallowed hard since I knew that from time to time I would have to act the role of gatekeeper, putting the reins on a desired future expenditure. Bill said he trusted me to take care of the family finances and when we occasionally hit a financial roadblock, we would sit down and work through it together.

Like Bill and I, Robert and Carolyn were able to reach an understanding that led to the creation of their own family value system.

When the planning of a wedding begins, so many issues – big and small – come to bear that many of us can't anticipate how our individual family value systems will influence our choices and expectations. Carolyn demonstrated that patience and understanding were the best remedies for financial jitters and insecurity about the future. Wouldn't it be great if all couples could handle differences with such honesty and tact ahead of time? I have a hunch that Robert and Carolyn will do just fine together.

Chapter 3

Parental Power Plays

I often work with brides and grooms of multicultural or mixed religious heritages seeking a way to have interfaith ceremonies, without offending either side of their families. But sometimes the parents and extended family members are adamant that certain aspects of the processional and format of the wedding ceremony reflect their own individual religious or cultural preferences. They may completely disregard the wishes of the bride and groom, an especially touchy situation if the parents are the primary financial sponsors for the wedding ceremony and reception.

Sometimes the extent of the rift doesn't become clear until the final planning meeting or the rehearsal after each family has had several months to do their back-room negotiating and arm-twisting. Everyone seems to have an opinion on how things should run, especially if the wedding is taking place in a non-religious setting. I have found that weddings held at a hotel, banquet center, or a rented space can give rise to alternative thinking and unexpected demands.

At a ceremony rehearsal when I find myself confronted with opposing convictions from family and wedding party members I have to become less the consultant and more the referee. Two stories come to mind that speak to the challenges that can arise with conflicting beliefs and opinions.

Margret and Alpert

Both weddings were held at a popular banquet center known for its nice surroundings. Our first bride Margret, a Catholic, was marrying Alpert, her Jewish groom. They had agreed on a Jewish ceremony. Alpert's dad had passed away a little under a year before the planned nuptials. The mother of the groom, Sarah, came to our final conference at the groom's condo to discuss the wedding day timeline and ceremony. She was contributing to the wedding budget by covering all the food and beverage fees, a decidedly large chunk of the wedding budget.

The bride and her father were present for this final conference too. The bride's parents were separated and the brides' mother was not living locally and was not present or actively participating in the planning, nor was she contributing financially. The father of the bride had bought his daughter's wedding gown and veil along with paying for the rehearsal dinner. The groom, on his own, was taking care of the rest of the expenses.

I came to the meeting with no pre-conceived ideas other than the processional order for a Jewish wedding according to the wishes of the bride and groom. I was reviewing the wedding day schedule of events with everyone in the room when we came to a surprising impasse.

I had begun writing down the names of each processional participant when the mother of the groom mentioned that her brother Mark, the uncle of the groom, would need to be seated next to her in the front row since she wanted him to walk both her son and herself down the aisle, now that she was widowed.

Suddenly, Alpert interrupted his mom with, "What made you think I wanted Uncle Mark to walk us down the aisle?" According to Jewish tradition, the groom is usually escorted down the aisle with his mother on his right and his father on his left. The groom's mom Sarah assumed that it only made sense for her brother to take the place of her late husband and walk down with them both.

Wow, Alpert unleashed a few remarks that really surprised me. He told his mom that even though Uncle Mark had been very supportive to her after his dad passed away, he never felt close to his uncle and that it would be meaningless for him to try to take the place of his father, even momentarily as a part of the processional. Alpert went on to say that there was no way he was going to walk down the aisle with his uncle. After a few minutes of back-and-forth remarks between Alpert and Sarah, Alpert's mother admitted that having her brother help walk her down the aisle with her son would make the loss of her husband a little easier to handle.

Margret (the bride) and her dad had been silent during the exchange between Alpert and his mom. I could tell by Margret's downturned head that she wanted to be anywhere else but sitting in between her fiancé and future mother-in-law.

I stepped in and offered an option that seemed to solve the problem luckily. I said, "Why don't we have Uncle Mark escort your mom from the building's glass doors where the processional begins to the first row of chairs at the back of the aisle. Uncle Mark would leave Sarah momentarily and continue to walk to his seat in the front row.

Alpert could begin walking out of the same doors once Uncle Mark and his mom were a few paces in front of him and would follow them until his mother and Uncle Mark reached the back row of chairs. Alpert would shortly join his mom so they could walk together the rest of the way to the Chuppah surrounded by their seated family and friends.

Sarah would be waiting under the Chuppah where parents of the bride and groom traditionally stand during the ceremony. That seemed to solve the dilemma. Both Alpert and Sarah were willing to compromise to make it work out for everyone, even though they were really both insistent on getting their way at the start of our meeting.

Feelings run deep in these situations and at least Alpert and his mom found a way to allow each other to have something of what they each wanted for the processional.

Lidia and Sam

Our next couple, Lidia and Sam, found themselves faced with a very different situation. In this case, the parents of the bride were adamant that their daughter would have a traditional Jewish ceremony with their rabbi and rejected the family of the groom's wish to have their parish priest give a blessing at the ceremony. The parents of the bride made it very clear that their daughter would be standing on the right side facing the Chuppah without being open to discuss the matter with the groom or his parents. In a Jewish ceremony the groom stands with his men on the left side of the aisle with their backs to the guests.

Sam was raised Catholic and was used to standing on the right side of the altar just as his five older brothers had done in their church weddings. Even though this change was a definite departure for him, being married outside the church and to a woman with another faith, he was open to standing on the left side of the Chuppah. His mom and dad were confused as to why their son would be standing on the left of the bride instead of the right side. After I explained the passage in Hebrew readings where it mentions the role of the bride to be on the right side of her husband, they nodded and said nothing further at the rehearsal.

As far as I could tell, there hadn't been much communication between the parents of the bride and groom prior to the rehearsal. The parents of the groom, Elizabeth and David, just went along where I told them to go during the processional practice until it was time for the both sets of parents to stand under the Chuppah. They declined to stand and said they would be sitting with their other relatives in the first row of chairs. The parents of the bride did not respond when the parents of the groom sat down during the rehearsal. It was clear the parents of the groom were less than enthusiastic about this ceremony and chose to sit in silence.

Looking back now, I shouldn't have been surprised about the friction between parents after my one and only meeting with the mother of the bride about a month before the wedding day.

I met the mother of the bride at the banquet center where the ceremony was to take place to go over the final details needed for the ceremony and to establish the schedule of events for the wedding day leading up to the ceremony. The mother of the bride, Brenda, made it clear that she was making all the major decisions regarding the wedding and her daughter would only meet me at the rehearsal. She said she understood she had to have a coordinator for the wedding day according to the rules of the banquet center, but she wasn't happy about the extra expense. The banquet center had recommended me along with a few others. Apparently her husband was the one that signed the contract with the banquet center where it stated the requirement to have a coordinator for the rehearsal and ceremony. Begrudgingly, she went along with the requirement and hired me.

We had agreed in writing at our initial meeting that I would be paid the remaining 50 percent of the coordinating fee on rehearsal night, relieving anyone of the responsibility of remembering to have a check ready during the flurry of wedding day activities.

On the rehearsal night the mother of the bride arrived visibly distant and nervous. She paced back and forth in the foyer of the banquet center waiting for her husband and daughter to appear. She did not engage in conversation with anyone. When her husband arrived she introduced me to her husband and daughter and then left to show her daughter where she would be standing for the ceremony.

I was about to ask for the final balance from the father of the bride before we began the rehearsal when he said something that just took my breath away. To this day, I can't decide if he was kidding or was speaking the truth. "Tobey," he said, "I will double your fee if you can find a way for my daughter not to marry her fiancé tomorrow."

I was totally stunned that he would approach a stranger like me and say such a thing, even if he was kidding. My first reaction was to laugh and call him a big kidder, but his look was dead serious. With a smile on my face I made it clear to him that the decision to get married was out of my control. The father shrugged his shoulders and said, "I tried," and we began the rehearsal practice. After that encounter I totally forgot to ask for my final payment.

On the wedding day, the bride arrived on time with her entourage of bridesmaids to help her dress. The mother of the bride was nowhere to be found. Just minutes before beginning separate photos before the ceremony, the parents of the bride arrived dressed and prepared to take photos.

During the last of the separate photos for the bridal side I approached the mother of the bride, Brenda, for the final payment. She said she forgot her checkbook and she would send me a check on Monday. I politely mentioned that we had time since her home was just a short distance away to go and get it, according to the terms of our agreement. She just said it would be very inconvenient and walked off to her daughter's changing room. I didn't push it, but I knew that I better talk to her early Monday morning to make sure she put the check in the mail.

It was time to line up for the procession and I reminded everyone of where they would be standing for the ceremony now that the Chuppah was in place. The oldest brother of the groom was the best man and I reminded him to stand on the left front side of the Chuppah as we had practiced it the night before.

I guess his nerves got to him and he landed on the right side of the Chuppah instead of the left. I told the other groomsmen to walk to the left side and just motion for the best man to join them, but they didn't listen to me either. It didn't dawn on me until after the ceremony that the mother of the groom had probably told her sons to stand on the other side of the Chuppah to satisfy at least one of her traditions. What could I do if they all followed suit? In her mind perhaps it wasn't that big of a deal logistically, but it would prove to be a mitigating factor in the mother of the bride's refusal to pay me the final balance of my fee.

No one said anything to me on the night of the wedding. On Monday morning the mother of the bride accused me of ruining the ceremony by not having the men stand on the correct side. I thought to myself, why is she blaming me when she was within earshot when I reminded everyone when and where to position themselves for the ceremony. I couldn't help feeling she was just making excuses because she didn't want her daughter to marry the groom and she resented the fact she had to pay for a ceremony coordinator.

I told her that since the photographer shot the images of the ceremony with film, it was easy to reverse the negatives and have her album with the groom standing on the left side. She scoffed at my suggestion and said, "That doesn't change what actually happened on the wedding day."

She refused to take my calls after that and when she complained to the management of the location, they reminded her that one of their staff was right there next to me, assisting me, and had heard me remind everyone of where they needed to be standing at the Chuppah.

There really wasn't anything more the owner of the banquet center could do to persuade the mother of the bride to pay me since I was performing as an independent contractor. Because the banquet center was so pleased with the way I handled myself during this incident, they gave my name out as often as they could for the next several years.

To cut corners and save some money, many clients of the banquet center hired friends to act as coordinators, causing unnecessary glitches because of their inexperience and lack of knowledge of event planning.

I was fortunate when it came to my own marriage to Bill. My florist was also a practicing wedding coordinator and conducted our rehearsal the night before the wedding. Even though we were of different faiths, Bill was comfortable with standing on the left side to honor my Jewish tradition and his father, a retired Baptist minister, even sipped from the glass of wine the Rabbi offered him. Little did the rabbi know it was the first time Bill's father ever tasted wine.

To stave off future problems with mandatory coordinators at the banquet facility, the center decided to employ their own in-house coordinators and made the service a part of their event packages.

I will always be grateful to the banquet center owners for their faith in me and for their support over the years. Even though there were some difficult moments working with parents and families members insisting on having things their way, I look back fondly on those beginning years as the perfect training ground to understand the motivation behind and lengths to which people will go to make sure their deeply held religious and cultural traditions will be honored.

Chapter 4

Teamwork at it's Best!

Even today as weddings unfold in real time on Instagram, Twitter, and Facebook, capturing what is happening minute by minute, it isn't until the professional wedding album or video is viewed that the day's memories completely gel for the couple and their families.

From the pre-ceremony getting-ready shots to the father of the bride seeing his daughter for the first time in her gown, the future emotional memoir begins. When the groom's moistened eyes gaze at his beautiful bride making her way down the aisle toward him, he realizes all the time and effort to achieve this apex of passion and tradition was worth it.

For me, it's the moment the ceremony begins that makes all the hours of preparation and the stress of meeting deadlines melt away; only then do the lasting memories begin for me.

When I am privileged to view the finished album or video with the newlyweds, we are revisiting not only the special moments of the wedding day, but also the combined teamwork of family members and wedding services whose efforts together create those memories preserved forever.

The wedding I'm sharing here had been a long and eventful day. It came together in large part by the efforts of the very capable parents of the bride, Judy and Sam, who tried to move things along while their daughter, Jeannie, and her fiancé, Carl, were crazy busy with their law practices, while also managing the renovation of their newly purchased home.

Judy and Sam were always there to support their daughter and be present whenever Jeannie and Carl needed their opinions or presence at meetings. With a lot of experience organizing special events under their belts, Judy and Sam, now retired, had the time to focus on their daughter's wedding.

Understandably, however, Jeannie and Carl wanted the wedding to reflect their own personalities, so some of the decision-making just had to wait until they could steal time away from their offices and home projects.

I am repeatedly struck by how often I encounter couples who have taken on three major projects. For Jeannie and Carl it was planning a wedding, buying and fixing up their first home, and for Jeannie, in particular, being promoted to partner at her law firm.

Both parents and bride and groom had high expectations and were used to being in the driver's seat in their professions. It wasn't always easy for them to let go and defer to others, even those who provided expert advice.

Operating under a mid-level planning service agreement that reserved the major decisions for the bride and her parents, there was only so much I could do ahead of the wedding. Everyone was fine with the division of labor, but no one could predict the intricacies and depth of feelings that arise when there are hundreds of smaller decisions that have to be made in quick succession to pull the grand wedding day off without a hitch in less than six months.

Jeannie tried to be very methodical in her approach to planning her wedding, thoroughly researching all services before making a final decision. I usually suggest a few options for services per category and anticipate that my client will meet with each service under one category and within a couple of weeks, make a selection as to which service will be a part of their wedding team. With Jeannie and Carl's over booked lives, I found myself biting my nails trying to keep services from taking other jobs while waiting for final decisions from Jeannie and Carl.

The deadline for selecting the invitations was closing in when Jeannie asked me if she would need to make final decisions on the invitation at our first meeting with the stationer. I told her that she wasn't obligated to make a decision on the spot, but hopefully she would find something she liked at the stationer and be able to work out basic wording, color and style. She could then take a couple of weeks to work out the fine points and review a proof before going to print.

After three hours at our first invitation meeting, I realized that while I may have been the mortar that held the event planning together, it was the experience and dedication to excellence from so many of the wedding services like the stationer, that would be pivotal in making this wedding come together.

About six weeks out from the wedding I sat down with Jeannie and Carl for our final major conference and they realized even though the big decisions were completed, many loose ends remained before their wedding day, particularly the logistical coordination of multiple simultaneous events on the wedding day.

Here's a quick rundown of the pre ceremony line up of activities:

Two separate beauty salons would be servicing the ladies, who then had to get back to the hotel for a brunch in the bride's room where the women would begin the dressing ritual.

At the same time, there was an early morning basketball game for the men followed by a separate lunch at a favorite deli. From there, the men would travel to the bride and groom's new house to clean up and dress for the wedding ceremony. This was definitely not going to be your standard cookie-cutter wedding day.

A total of five locations were photographed which seemed daunting to me, but James, our photographer, worked out with me how much time he would need per location. My scheduling chops were put to the test for sure. We assembled an informal fleet of family vehicles, limos and trucks to transport everyone where they needed to be at the specified times. This part of the day was to wrap up at two o'clock in the afternoon, leaving just enough time for everyone to get dressed and get to the church without the bride and groom seeing each other before the ceremony at three.

While all this was going on, part of my team was at the restaurant changing over the décor and setting up for the wedding reception with the catering staff. One of my assistants was also overseeing the set-up of the park across the street from the church where guests would be entertained following the receiving line at the close of the ceremony, while the wedding party was being photographed. The interlude in the park was planned to keep the guests from arriving too early at the restaurant where the staff needed time to complete the changeover from lunch to a special event set-up, giving the florist enough time to set up floral arrangements and the photographer being able to do the post ceremony group photos.

To entice the guests to exit the church quickly we hired a mariachi band to lead them out of the sanctuary and across the street to a shady park for some refreshing cold drinks and ice cream freezes to stave off the 95 plus degree temperature anticipated.

On the day of the wedding the logistics and the number of activities got a little tricky at times.

The groomsmen were held up getting to the church due to a fire truck blocking an intersection, cutting short the time the photographer had to take photos of the groomsmen in their tuxes at the church. Somehow James sandwiched in time after the ceremony before we headed to the restaurant to claim those must have images.

My praise goes to the bridesmaids. They were loyal friends who soothed the bride through her upset stomach, while comforting her and attending to her every need before dressing themselves. They stayed calm when their hems began unraveling as they dressed and were patient while my assistant and I pinned, sewed and glued sequins back onto their dresses.

Kudos also to the florist, Michael, who volunteered to make two different bouquets for the bride so her flowers would always look fresh in photos over the span of twelve hours of activities, refusing to charge her for the second bouquet. Michael artfully selected alternate blossoms for the second bouquet that would be hearty enough to withstand the nearly triple-digit temperatures without changing the overall look Jeannie was after for the reception.

His long-standing relationships with linen suppliers really paid off when Jeannie had a change of heart a week before the wedding and requested different linen colors.

When the mariachis were lost and went to the wrong church, I called the entertainment company representative, Mark, who went the extra distance to find the wrong church. He drove his car to them and then they followed him to the correct church.

The mother of the bride had her heart set on staging the grand photos of the entire 175-person guest-list in the park on the steps of the raised area near the covered veranda. James, our photographer, had visited the park earlier in the week and decided the step area would work. But when the day arrived James said the light was uneven and it was his professional opinion that another area would be better.

Even with my urging to follow the photographer's solution, the mother of the bride insisted on the steps for the group photo. The photographer, my assistant and I moved all 175 of the guests to the steps of the veranda within a few minutes. Jeannie wanted her dress bustled at that very moment to hide the unavoidable staining on her train from the undetected damp spots of soil. I didn't want to delay the photos, especially in the hot afternoon sun, so I crouched down behind Jeannie as she and Carl posed with their guests, trying to fix the bustle at the same time while trying not to be seen in the photos. I felt so badly because I tried to contort my body to half its volume, but my bulky 5'10" frame didn't cooperate and I'm sure the photographer had to Photoshop my elbows and knees out of a few shots.

The last leg of this journey would be the guests' promenade on foot to the restaurant a couple of blocks away for dinner and dancing. The mariachis would walk alongside, serenading the guests who were offered paper parasols and flip-flops to ease the hot journey and allow the ladies to slip out of their high heels.

We knew not all the guests would opt for walking and it was a good thing since the church coordinator informed us right before the ceremony that there was a program at the church in another adjoining building following our ceremony and they needed the parking spaces we had taken up with our cars.

The restaurant owner even helped us out with the hot weather, since the dinner reception was all outside, and found a way to gather more excursion boats for us, giving more guests a chance to cool off and enjoy the lake right next to the restaurant at sundown too.

I swear, our photographer, James, was as much an athlete as a photographer on the wedding day. Five separate locations required photo coverage. The rest of the time James and his video crew were bobbing and weaving through tables under the canopy of umbrellas, avoiding waiters holding drink orders and animated guests talking with their hands. Artfully, he grabbed shots of the cake and table centerpieces, while capturing the ambience of the wedding guests enjoying the evening.

To James, shooting in the moment was his way of making the most of what was available to him in timing and lighting. He maneuvered effortlessly around natural obstacles while fulfilling spontaneous photo requests of the families and friends throughout the evening.

I could stop here and you would know that the photographer did a great job, and that would have been great, but there is so much more to the story. If any one wedding service or wedding party member had failed to perform their tasks and duties in a timely manner, a domino effect could have ensued, spelling disaster.

Jeannie had her heart set on whipped cream icing for her wedding cake. Knowing how delicate whipping cream is in hot weather, the bakery supplying the cake made our wedding the last delivery of the day and delivered it partially frozen so it could sit out longer than normal. Again the catering staff stepped in and hand-carried the multi-layered wedding cake from inside the air-conditioned restaurant to the outside table just in time for the cake cutting to preserve the integrity of the cake.

And then there was the DJ. He analyzed the sound needs perfectly and made sure we were able to hear the speeches by providing a wireless mic to be used outside during dinner while his set up was inside the restaurant ready for after dinner dancing to avoid extra charges for a second system. He calculated the distance and placement of all speakers during dinner to keep the sound clear and not interrupt the signal.

He also filled in song selections when Jeannie and Carl couldn't make up their minds for special party tunes. Throughout the evening he set and maintained the pace of the party, thrilling the crowd when he stayed for an extra hour past the conclusion time.

For me, this wedding day felt like a marathon for my feet that stretched over twelve hours without a minute of downtime except a few moments to sit and scarf down the restaurant's delicious offerings — and I mean delicious.

The catering crew was particularly attentive to the bride and groom, anticipating their every desire. At the end of the evening the catering manager wouldn't even take a tip for the overtime that had accrued. The owner insisted on my crew sharing it since my gals who stayed on really helped his crew during the set up and throughout the evening.

How fortunate we all were that the parents of the bride and our wedding couple selected a group of seasoned services that knew each other well. Working together like a well-tuned engine, they each instinctively knew what the others were doing and what needed to happen to get the job done at any given moment. Their professionalism and dedication made the difference between just getting through the day and creating special, everlasting memories for the wedding families and their attendees.

Chapter 5

The Hits and Misses

Most of the time I am able to sense an impending disaster at a wedding in time to take precautionary measures. But once the worst has happened, I am responsible for cleaning up the mess and doing what I can to lessen the disappointment for the couple and their loved ones.

Those are the misses: The unfortunate lapses that seem so awful at the time, the embarrassing moments I wish I could take back instantly. But in reality, no one is perfect and sometimes I am guilty of a slip of the tongue, a missed cue, or the unintentional loss of something of value.

This chapter is intended as neither a drive down the lane of bad memories nor a series of pats on my own back for saving the day. What I hope to convey here is a sense of gratitude for all that goes well along with a lesson in putting safeguards into place that will give us the best chance to succeed whether we are a service, guest, or client.

Here is one triumph and one trial — at the same wedding

Many years ago I had the privilege of working with a beauty queen. She was gorgeous with stunning green eyes and amber locks; there was a grace about her that was rare. Sylvia came to my home office with her sister and mother, bubbling over with enthusiasm and anticipation for the best day of her life to come in just a few months. We must have spoken a good two hours about the wedding day, what it would look like to the guests and feel like to the bride.

She was seriously focused when talking about the atmosphere she was intending to create with the décor, linens, lighting and accessories. It was obvious Sylvia had taken a great amount of time and energy to make sure all the accessories were coordinated in color, material and style. I soon realized I had a family of perfectionists in front of me. I had to find a way to compliment Sylvia and her family for all their hard work and establish trust and attention to every detail that was important to them. To reinforce that point, I showed them images of a few weddings that featured a strong theme and attention to detail to assure them I understood what was important in creating the atmosphere and pace they wanted to experience on the wedding day.

Since I was mainly hired to make the wedding day run smoothly, Sylvia took pains to tell me where she wanted everything to go at the site. I had three pages of these details just in the initial conference. I noted, however, that while this amber beauty had selected a location with lovely grounds, the reception room and food really didn't measure up to her high standards she had expressed for everything else.

It wasn't long before I figured out why she had selected this particular location. The cost of the room, food and beverages was a good deal lower than some of the major hotels in the surrounding area, allowing Sylvia to allocate more money toward the décor and details that were so important to her. She was definitely not alone in her thoughts and priorities. Many clients have done the same over the years.

Sylvia wanted her guests to be dazzled by the ambiance and if it meant her guests had less elaborate appetizers or call drinks instead of premium or deluxe brands, so be it. It came down to Sylvia opting for a five-star visual experience with a three-star food and beverage offering.

One striking element of the wedding would be the centerpiece of the reception room, an eight-tiered wedding cake with a custom-blown glass topper. Even though the total guest count would be approximately 180, Sylvia's cake could have served nearly 300 guests. Some brides elect to have some faux layers added to the cake to heighten the drama of the presentation. This cake was real through and through. In her mind, there would be enough cake to celebrate a whole year of celebrations. Lace embellishments in royal icing, with pearls and crystal drops acting as gathering points for the lacey fondant icing on the cake made for a richly textured cake, mirroring the sparkling finishes on Sylvia's own wedding gown.

When it came time to place the 24-inch-tall glass topper on the cake, neither the baker nor anyone from the catering staff wanted to take responsibility for doing the deed. The catering staff eyed and measured and finally declared that there was about two inches of ceiling clearance for the glass masterpiece.

My heart started to pound because it was becoming apparent that yours truly was going to have to woman up and make it happen. I surveyed the obstacles and determined my course of action. I would have to climb on a chair and then step up onto the edge of the table where I would reach above the five-foot high cake and delicately slide the glass piece into place, avoiding the low points in the coffered ceiling.

One of the servers kindly took my hand and helped me from the chair cushion onto the surface of the round 72-inch table, while another server had my back in case I lost my balance. I didn't hear anyone talking. I was totally focused on getting that cake top onto the cake. As another server handed me the glass cake topper to place, I kept thinking, thank heavens the topper was made of very thin blown art glass weighing just a few ounces.

Once the deed was done, I heaved a sigh of relief and gingerly stepped down from the table. It took three of us to achieve the task with a half dozen servers looking on in silent prayer.

After a moment of elation, I paused with the thought, O.M.G., somehow after the bride and groom cut the cake we have to remove the topper without the spectacle of me climbing on the table again. We needed to make sure the guests were all dancing and not watching us disassemble this flour, sugar, and butter gem.

When the DJ arrived to set up I shared with him what we had gone through to put the topper on the cake and asked if he would work his magic to get the dancing started immediately following the cutting of the cake so my gymnastic performance didn't steal the show.

Scary thoughts kept running through my head. I prayed that the dancing guests wouldn't get too frenetic and start jumping. Vibrations have been known to affect a cake in ways I don't even want to remember. Let's just say, I've seen my share of cascading layers and tumbling objects of art due to the impact of gyrating guests a full ten feet away, a situation that can be much worse when you are not stabilized on the building's ground floor.

The good news is we got through the evening with the glass topper intact and I was able to remove it discreetly while guests danced. I retrieved the original corrugated oblong box from under the covered gift table, re-boxed the topper and returned it to its place next to all the other accessory boxes now filled with the guest book, toasting goblets, ring pillow and other precious mementos. The only objects that were exposed on the top of the table were wedding gifts from the guests.

I have learned that it is always a good idea to task one trustworthy person with a single vehicle to pack up the gifts and deliver them to the designated home. This cuts down on confusion and mishaps. At the end of the evening a friend of the family was on hand with his truck to transport the gifts, along with a maid of honor, to monitor the items to be taken.

I opened each box for the maid of honor to inspect so she could verify that all accessories were accounted for. Then we loaded up the truck and thought we were good to go.

A couple of weeks later I got a lovely thank you call from the bride, back from her honeymoon. After her compliments for a wonderful event, she asked me if I knew where the cake topper was since they searched everywhere and couldn't find it. I was dumbfounded that the topper was missing. How could that happen? Every precaution was taken to make sure that the accessories were saved, boxed and stored together and then reviewed with the maid of honor before being loaded onto the truck — I was on hand helping every step of the way.

After retracing my steps mentally, I came up with a possible explanation, one I didn't think anyone would like but I believed may actually have happened. When I first unwrapped the box and removed the cake topper I was surprised at the large size of the topper because the box itself was so lightweight. Thinking back now, if someone would have handed me the box with the topper in it, I might have thought the topper had already been removed — I might have thought I was holding an empty box with a lot of tissue inside.

Perhaps some family member who helped unpack the gifts at the home of the mother of the bride thought the box was empty and tossed it. What if, while I was outside helping load the truck, a well-meaning catering staffer began cleaning up the area a bit prematurely and saw what he thought was an empty box due to its feather weight and tossed it out to be helpful?

A couple days later I got a call from a police detective asking me again what I remember doing with the cake topper. I found out that the topper was valued at $500. I felt terrible that an object of such value had somehow disappeared. An offer to take a polygraph test and assist the police department in any way possible ended my involvement in the incident.

I realized after that evening that it is necessary to clearly label all packages whether opened or not with a note indicating to saves boxes whether empty or full for the bride. I also insist on having a designated responsible party review the gifts with me and initial each item checked in my presence.

There is no perfect solution, but as guests, clients, and wedding services, we all should be willing to tell the host or someone in charge if they see anything left behind on a guest table, in the bathrooms, or if they notice someone in the event room who doesn't look like they belong.

Epilogue:

Seven years later I got a call from the same family to help with the younger daughter's wedding. Even though I wasn't available for the wedding date, I still felt a tug at my heartstrings wanting to have solved the mystery of the missing cake topper.

Chapter 6

Is This Moment Really Happening?

When it comes to wedding disasters, it's the one you've never encountered, the wholly unimaginable and unpredictable that's going to throw you off balance. I reached a point some time ago where I thought I'd seen it all, but now I know better.

Things can happen at a wedding or in the moments leading up to one that can't be predicted or avoided because they can't be imagined. It's these unpredictable moments that call for the best in us as wedding services, guests, and bridal couple to rise to the occasion, hang in there, and figure something out to go on with the event.

Here are a few of those head-spinning moments.

Frozen in Time

The classical musicians had been playing contemporary love songs as guests entered and were seated on the brick and wrought iron terrace overlooking the green fairways below. The golden orange leaves of the tree line framed the hillsides in the distance. This suburban country club was the perfect backdrop to Barbara and Cliff's autumn wedding. All had gone well prior to the wedding processional. We were on time and the last of the guests were making their way to their seats. The ushers gave me the cue that there were no more guests to be seated and now it was time for the music to change for the formal wedding ceremony processional.

I had just completed lining up the wedding party. With the final check of the bridesmaids and groomsmen's attire, we were ready to begin. Even the ring bearer and flower girls stopped swaying their pillow and baskets from side to side, realizing it was time to focus and wait for their cue to walk down the four steps ahead and turn left down the aisle to their waiting parents in the first row of chairs.

I asked Barbara to take a few steps forward as the wedding party moved ahead. I just needed a little more room to straighten out her train and veil behind her, but she just stood still. I came closer to her to give her a final few encouraging words as I do with all my brides when possible, when I realized she was just staring straight ahead like she was in some kind of trance. I asked her to take a few deep breaths. Finally I saw her chest move up and down, but all she could say to me is, "Tobey, I can't move. I don't know that I can do this." I knew I had to work fast to help this bride down the aisle if she still wanted to get married.

Nearly forty years old, Barbara was a very independent woman who was having her first and hopefully only wedding. No time could be carved out of the moment for even a brief conversation about her feelings and apprehensions. Her dad, standing rigidly beside her like a petrified tree, wasn't helping matters either. He didn't utter a sound.

Instinctively I came around to face her and I put both of my arms on her shoulders gently and asked her to look into my eyes. I told her I wouldn't let her get married if she answered "no" to any of the three questions I was about to ask her. In a split second I blurted out the first three thoughts that came into my mind.

Do you love this man?

Do you trust him with your life?

Do you think he will be a good father if you have children?

I was hoping for honest and sincere responses from Barbara. After three yeses I said, "You are ready to get married."

Away she went down the aisle with her dad. I will always remember Barbara and Cliff, not only for that moment of intense drama, but as much for the odd reason she gave for having selected me, partly because her cat was named Tobey.

Cathy and Robert's Shrinking Guest List

When I first met with Cathy and Robert, the sky was the limit in planning the wedding of their dreams. Cathy, a busy downtown real estate agent and Robert, a prominent CPA, knew their taste level came at a significant price and they were okay spending what it would take to make their dream wedding a reality.

They selected a beautiful spot in the hills overlooking Malibu. The mansion was made of stone and the gardens were to die for. Tall pine trees stood on one side of the property while a flat central lawn was ringed in white blooming rose bushes. With a view of the Pacific Ocean, this site was hard to beat for beauty, comfort, and elegance.

Their guest list was a healthy 150 plus with a possible cap of 200. Cathy had a really large family traveling from the Northwest. Robert was an East Coaster from a small tight-knit family. As a couple they had loads of friends and professional colleagues they wanted to invite. Robert was a bit younger than Cathy with two children under five years of age while Cathy, in her late thirties, was getting married for the first time.

Every time we got together for a planning meeting I couldn't believe how attentive and supportive Robert was toward Cathy. It was as if he treasured every word that came out of her mouth. He had proposed to her during a lunch he arranged on the beach, having hired a plane to fly overhead trailing a banner that asked, Will you marry me? He had even written her poetry on several occasions prior to their engagement. I was in awe of his admiration for her.

It was rare that Robert ever said no to something Cathy really wanted, even if it meant going over budget slightly. In many ways, Cathy and Robert were a dream couple. They were decisive when they needed to be and made time for meetings not always convenient for them professionally.

We were about eight weeks out from their wedding day when Cathy called me fighting back tears. I said, "What in the world is wrong? You sound awful." Cathy went on to tell me that when she didn't receive the printed invitations she discovered that Robert had failed to pay the bill.

When she asked him about it, he revealed that when he left his accounting firm recently to go out on his own, he was counting on several key accounts to follow him to his new firm and was disappointed when they failed to do so. He kept thinking he would get enough new clients to make up the difference, but that didn't happen. Robert told her he just couldn't face the fact that he wasn't able to provide the kind of wedding they both wanted.

My heart went out to Cathy since she had been kept in the dark and led to believe that everything was fine. She was at a loss as to how to handle the situation. On the one hand she didn't want to get mad at Robert because he always worked so hard, but she was frustrated that he didn't trust her enough to share his business setbacks, which now jeopardized their wedding plans. I told Cathy that it was time for us to meet and put our heads together to figure out a way to lower the budget without hurting the quality of the wedding.

I knew that we had to do something quickly since wedding service payments were coming due and wedding invitations normally go out about eight weeks prior to the wedding date. Hopefully, we could make adjustments where possible to make Cathy and Robert's situation better than it seemed at that moment.

When we met I suggested that we shrink the guest list to 100 guests instead of trying to lower the service packages of the photographer, videography and other set service fees. Initially that idea went over like a lead balloon. Cathy rolled her eyes and Robert just couldn't look me in the eye and shook his head from side to side in the negative.

After I mentioned that the services they selected had given them great values and their fees could not be reduced without losing much of the character of their wedding, they started realizing that lowering the guest count was our best way to make sure they had the money to pay for everything dear to them both and would sacrifice having some of their local friends and distant relatives that they rarely see.

I told them the caterer would be willing to lower the minimum to 100 guests without penalty on the per person fee for this smaller guest count. We would be saving nearly $25,000 on their entire wedding budget, but for Cathy and Robert this reality check was a tough blow. They desperately wanted to keep their dream wedding alive.

Looking at Cathy, with Robert listening, I told her the important thing is that they are still getting married and they have found a way to keep the site and the services they really value. To Cathy, Robert was still the most romantic, giving man she could imagine marrying. He was the man of her dreams. It may sound corny but she really felt he was the prince charming who would take her to his castle and live happily ever after.

To help them through the process of choosing who would stay on the list and who would be dropped, I asked them to consider which guests they thought they would still feel as close to in five or ten years as they did today. Each guest they couldn't honestly answer yes to was removed from the list, seventy-five people in all. On the wedding day the final guest list totaled one hundred and ten. Their wedding day turned out to be amazing; all the fine touches they worked so hard to make possible were so enjoyed by all and helped make the wedding day memorable and special, even with the reduced guest list.

Road Blocks to a Wedding

The view from the canyon was magnificent. Rolling hills still green from the winter rains stretched out like a green carpet through which paths of scrub oaks and mustard seed meandered. Lizzie and John had chosen a friend's home with a spectacular ocean view for their wedding ceremony and reception.

They planned to have 130 to 140 guests and all the details seemed to be taken care of by the week of the wedding. Nearly 70 family members and friends were arriving in town on the Wednesday and Thursday before the wedding.

The location Lizzy and John selected may have not been the most centrally located, but being able to use the groom's friend's home instead of renting a comparable property saved $10,000 to $12,000 on the wedding. Lizzie and John continued to watch their spending while still making their guests feel special by including them in as many wedding week activities as possible. They made sure their directions were easy to follow to aid guests who were navigating locations in Santa Monica and Malibu, CA for the first time. Most of the guests from out of town were staying in four major hotels in Santa Monica, about 40 to 50 minutes down the coast from the wedding site.

Having most of guests staying near each other saved the need for transportation arrangements for the rehearsal dinner in Santa Monica. All the guests were able to walk to the restaurant from their hotels.

To make the wedding party feel special, Lizzie and John elected to have a special toast and appetizers at the ceremony practice up at the wedding site before they joined everyone else in Santa Monica for an informal buffet dinner on a reserved restaurant patio overlooking the Pacific Ocean. Inviting all the out-of-town guests to mingle and to get to know each other before the wedding day gave everyone a feeling of inclusion and let them know Lizzie and John appreciated their presence.

Everything was going great until I got a call from Laurie, the maid of honor, the next morning on the wedding day. She was staying in an inn in Malibu. The plan was to have the rest of the wedding party join her in her suite to do their hair and make up for the wedding day in a couple of hours. Laurie stated the problem simply: "We have no water."

Apparently there was a water main break somewhere between Santa Monica and Malibu and the city shut off the water all the way up the coast, including most of Malibu. I felt so badly for Lizzie and the entire wedding was now in jeopardy unless we could find water for the wedding site.

I told Laurie and Lizzie I would call one of the hotels in Santa Monica and arrange for a hotel room for just the wedding day and make sure the hair and make-up people were alerted to go to the hotel instead of the inn in Malibu. Between the Maid of Honor and myself we called the rest of the women and men in the wedding party to make sure they were aware of the water problem and they were grateful for the heads up.

Once the women had a place to get ready with running water, I turned my attention to getting bathrooms for the guests since it was likely that we wouldn't be able to use the home's bathrooms now. I called the caterer and she was on it so quickly; she would do her best to get mobile bathrooms delivered while bringing in drinking water. That was one big load off my mind.

Next, I needed to access the extent of the water problem. I couldn't get through to the water department so I called the Highway Patrol and they confirmed that all roads leading to Malibu would be closed to non-residents unless the driver had proof of a necessity to enter the area. There were at least three canyon roads and Pacific Coast Highway entrance points to Malibu. The highway patrol spokesperson said there would be units posted at all entry points to Malibu from the north, east, and south to check cars coming into the area. I asked if wedding invitations would be sufficient to grant access to Malibu. The officer on the phone said, "That should do it."

Well, this wedding came well before email and texting were the norm. How was I going to reach each guest to tell them to bring their invitation? It was very possible that many of the guests didn't have copies of their invitations because they planned to use the map and directions they received in a separate packet.

I called Jeff Ames, my good friend who was the DJ for the wedding day, to tell him and the other wedding services to bring copies of their contracts to show to the officers manning the check points later in the day. I emailed a copy of the invitation to Jeff and he was kind enough to make copies and send them to the various hotels' concierge departments while I got a mailing list from Lizzie and John and began calling the guests who were not staying at hotels to tell them they needed to provide proof that they were attending the wedding. Jeff and I were on the phone for three hours, but eventually we reached every guest.

Our plan worked; we only lost two guests out of 140 expected. Great teamwork, a little luck with the portable bathrooms, and we all managed to reach our destination. Thank God we had a lot of family that helped spread the word and looked after each other getting to the site so everyone could enjoy the day.

In life, things happen that we can't anticipate, imagine, or expect. Having contingency plans at the ready helps, but what saves the day in the end is the will and determination to do your best for those you are working with, while creating an atmosphere of cooperation and diligence to produce the best possible outcome. It won't come as any surprise to you that from Lizzie and John's wedding onward, I made it a practice to have all the preparations done before the rehearsal. Then, when a "day of emergency" arises, I'm not busy folding ceremony programs or delivering guest baskets to hotels, instead, I focus on attending to the critical situation at hand.

Chapter 7

What Every Bride Wants in a Dad

Before finally escorting his daughter down the aisle and giving her away to a son-in-law he hopes will be a good husband and dad, a father of the bride takes a journey of his own that is often under-appreciated. From the respective movie portrayals by Spencer Tracy and Steve Martin in the original and remake of the comedy, "The Father of the Bride," fathers have been depicted as men under siege, desperately trying to retain their stature in the family while being overwhelmed with changing mores and an often-unchecked assault on their bank accounts.

Some dads acquiesce: "Yes dear; anything you want, dear," while writing out yet another check. Others maintain a hawk-like vigil over every line item under consideration, keeping a tight grip on the purse strings.

Whether they're made out of cotton candy or tempered steel, over the years these fathers of daughters must steady themselves for the kaleidoscope of female trials, tribulations and triumphs. They will witness epic attention paid to training bras, fashion show luncheons, sweet sixteen parties and debutant balls as their little girls become young women, crafting their unique vision of the feminine mystique. There will be grand parties, emotional roller coasters and a spiritual quest as these daughters prepare to assume the traditional mantle of womanhood: Marriage.

It sometimes helps if the father of the bride grew up with sisters. These seasoned males have already learned the fine art of dashing in and out of showers just in time to avoid a steamy bathroom; they've learned to shave quickly and hide the razor so no red-nailed, eagle-eyed bandit will snatch it away for a quick swipe of her downy armpits.

They've learned to either hold it or take quick steps to the bushes out back to get the job done while their sisters straighten what was curly or curl what was straight to avoid a ticket from the fashion police.

Few fathers are prepared for their daughter's transformation from pigtails to perfectly coiffed do's. With the realization that the rainbow of wedding wishes has truly cost them a pot of gold, a father can perhaps find solace in a son-in-law gained who actually understands the difference between a hook shot, a forward pass and a squeeze play.

Fewer still are able to endure the full season of wedding day practice sessions; those marathon conferences where the minutia of dress and décor is sorted out and the wedding day logistics are scheduled in detail. I've seen many a dad excuse himself to watch TV or take the dog for a walk, which may be preferable to dozing off during an earnest discussion of the color of the cake frosting.

Dr. Barry, we will call him, was one in a million. He preferred to have us sit in the family room around the large square coffee table for these wedding talks that began nearly eighteen months prior to the wedding day. His wife, Genevieve, took the far corner of the couch next to the "wedding room" as they called it (this space could have been a chapter in itself), while the bride and her fiancé took the other end of the couch. Dr. Barry burrowed down into his worn leather club chair, his legs stretched out in front as he leaned back into a semi-reclined position.

The chair was his refuge as we went through the endless details about who walks with who, which toast happens when between culinary prompts in the evenings' scripted agenda, and then on to which top 40 dance tunes would be played while guests swiveled and bounced on the rented glossy white dance floor.

Dr. Barry took everything in stride. He let Genevieve chatter on and on: "How much is this going to cost? It doesn't it make sense to bring the votive candles, table numbers, etc. when we can just rent everything or pay someone else to make it."

At times it was exhausting, but Dr. Barry weathered all of the discussions until he decided it was time to issue a decree. It often went like this: "Genevieve, this is what we're doing. It's decided. No more discussion. On to the next topic."

Period. Exclamation point! Done.

After hanging her head low for a second or two, Genevieve simply moved to the next topic with as much passion and fervor as the previous issue and those to come, dissecting all the options, convinced that her viewpoint made the most sense.

One thing for sure, Dr. Barry couldn't wait to talk about the father/daughter dance. He wanted to make sure he got it right. His daughter, Darian, and he practiced for long intervals, swirling and spinning, twisting, and grooving to a medley of tunes they agreed would represent their decades together. From the time Darian was born she loved to have music playing when she went to sleep, when it was time to distract her on the potty seat, and when the boogieman was hiding in the closet just before bedtime prayers. Her father always supplied the tunes.

There had been countless trips back and forth to soccer practice that Dr. Barry managed to attend on Wednesday afternoons and evenings despite his busy schedule. Whether they won or lost, music blared from the station wagon filled with a team of sweaty pubescent gigglers.

Even though those days were long gone, replaced by, "I'll see you Dad on Monday night when I get back from Jeff's place," Dr. Barry still saw that little girl who used to stand on her daddy's loafers in her sock-covered feet and dance to Madonna's latest hit on the parquet floor of the family room.

When the wedding day came, our father of the bride was anxious to see his little girl in her wedding gown for the first time. It meant so much for him to be there even before the groom. Darian came out of the changing room at the ranch where the women were dressing and posed for her dad, bouquet in hand, just outside the large white stucco quarters.

The massive rustic oak door made Darian look small, reminding her father of his little girl standing outside the front door of her childhood home before her first communion nearly 20 years earlier.

Dr. Barry shed a few tears as he and his daughter followed the grass and stone pathway to the altar. Jeff watched as his future bride and father-in-law exchanged smiles and squeezed hands before he took his bride's hand and drew Darian toward him. Together they walked the extra few steps until they stood under the wrought-iron arch covered in white roses and lavender clusters. With the pastor's question the transition was complete: "Who gives this woman's hand in marriage?" "Her mother and I do," answered Dr. Barry, loud and clear.

With the celebration underway after the ceremony, the next highlight for Dr. Barry was the father/daughter dance traditionally performed at the close of the main course. But Dr. Barry wanted to go back in time and exercise an older custom: He would start the first dance with Darian, then allowing Jeff to cut in so the couple could finish the dance as husband and wife.

Once everyone was seated for dinner, the newlyweds appeared and were introduced as Mr. and Mrs. The couple then made their way to the sweetheart table waving at their cheering guests. Dr. Barry took the microphone and welcomed all the guests, especially Jeff and his family. He waxed poetic about having a son-in-law who understood the ritual of Monday night football and the necessity to get season tickets for Dodger home games while at the same time being patient enough to go window shopping with his new wife after a Friday night dinner date when the spirit moved her.

The tune, "I Loved You First" filled the air as Jeff brought Darian to the middle of the dance floor to join her dad. Father and daughter twirled, moved back and forth, and ended their dance with a dip they had recently planned rather than passing the dance to Jeff. The song ended as Darian bent down and kissed her dad on his right cheek.

Dr. Barry had been in a car accident just a few months before the wedding and had lost the use of his legs. His recovery had come as far as the doctors could hope for. Having that first dance, even in a wheelchair, with his daughter twirling him meant everything to them both.

Somehow all the details fretted over paled in comparison to the emotional high of Darian and her dad completing the father/daughter dance, commemorating a lifetime of loving memories shared between them.

Dr. Barry's front row seat next to the dance floor gave him a perfect view of Darian and Jeff enjoying the night's festivities. When it came time for Darian and Jeff to cut the cake and say a few words of thanks, Darian began by blowing a kiss to her dad for giving her the best night of her life and thanking her mom for working so hard to keep her eye on the bottom line.

By the time the last dance was done, Dr. Barry turned to me and said, "It went by too fast; it's all a blur to me."

"I know," I agreed. "When you are having fun, time flies by, but you will always have the photos and video to remind you of just how great the day turned out for everyone."

Chapter 8

A Lost Love and One Finally Found

I couldn't help but notice when I first met with John and Meg how much more he was tuned into the wedding talk than she. John apologized for their lateness due to a cocktail reception they had just come from for a client of his. Both of them seemed relaxed and feeling no pain from the libations they consumed at the reception. I offered them some coffee and they responded in the affirmative.

John quickly unloaded all the particulars of their pasts so I could understand their individual experiences and family relationships, as well as their present lifestyle. Meg seemed charmingly coy and reluctant to talk about herself in a personal way, while John reminisced about how they met and got engaged.

John, a busy advertising executive, seemed very thoughtful, wanting to establish a warm and open relationship as they conducted their initial interview with me to determine if I would be their choice for wedding planner. Meg, a freelance graphic artist, was so relaxed she propped up the loose pillows behind her neck and leaned back in the cushions of my brown velour 70's vintage couch as she listened to John talk about their upcoming wedding day. In contrast, John leaned forward and became more hyper and excited while sharing his ideas about the wedding and what they had accomplished so far.

When I asked which of the two of them would be my point person on all wedding matters, John and Meg answered in unison, "John." I said fine and we continued to talk about their big day.

With his decisive nature and eye for detail, John was the perfect client for me. We laughed when their guest list kept growing as John couldn't leave out a single client, long time neighbor, or work mate. Meg countered by adding old drinking buddies from college whom she hadn't spoken to in years and even a few old boyfriends she had dated briefly. I gave my usual speech about avoiding inviting old boyfriends and drinking buds, but Meg resisted, leaving them all on the list. Over time, it became clear to me that Meg didn't have a lot of current friends. Maybe being an independent contractor had something to do with that. She was always working and running to catch up on all things wedding related. She passed on having the ritual of a bridal shower too, relying on old childhood friends to shore up her list of attendees as if intimidated by John's much larger guest list.

As we got closer to the wedding day John began taking on some of tasks originally assumed by Meg who rarely called me and seemed content to let John make all the large and small decisions right up to the wedding day. Meg was behaving more like a bystander rather than the bride to me.

The wedding day started out perfectly. The set up and photos went well and John and Meg looked so happy. Meg was more outgoing than I'd ever seen her, laughing and really enjoying herself. She seemed not to have a care in the world.

During the early part of the day John approached me periodically and asked how things were going and if any loose ends still needed attention. I told him we were doing just fine and tried to get him to turn his entire focus on his lovely bride, Meg.

"Today you are the groom," I reminded him, "so take off your wedding hard hat, kick back, and enjoy yourself. You have definitely earned your keep as a groom, so it's time to have some fun!" John smiled broadly as if I had just granted him permission to live in the moment.

The sun was low in the sky as ushers began asking the guests to take their seats for the ceremony. There was a slight snap in the air. Good thing we had heaters for the dinner reception later. Temperatures can change quickly in a canyon and we were well prepared.

The procession began with John walking down the stone garden path accompanied by the wedding officiate. Hopeful that he had found the right woman, John carried himself with positive anticipation. He had reached the big 4-0 and was looking forward to having a family of his own.

I stood near Meg who was hanging out behind the garage waiting for me to cue her to walk down the path solo. She began cracking jokes and letting off steam. She seemed too relaxed — almost flip — to be taking these serious steps toward her future with John.

Seconds before the music cue Meg took a few puffs on a cigar that the groomsmen had just put down before walking ahead of her and the bridesmaids. When I offered her a breath mint she turned to me, drawing the cigar back and forth in her mouth, and said, "Just practicing for later tonight."

Throwing her head back in a big belly laugh, she surrendered the cigar. Perhaps this was her way of casting off a case of hidden jitters. After all, her first marriage had ended just a couple of years prior with a lot of acrimony attached to the split. Her last comment to me before walking down the aisle took me by surprise when she said, "John makes my life too easy."

As the ceremony got underway, I heard a vehicle in the distance making its way up the hillside parallel to the ceremony setting. I was hoping security would radio or text me before letting anyone up the hill during the ceremony to avoid distractions.

Unfortunately, I was unable to pick up the call from the driver who was in charge of the courtesy van, possibly due to a weak radio signal in the canyon. The van arrived with a late guest (we will call him Charlie), who stormed frantically out of the vehicle and rushed toward me, nervously running his fingers through his salt-and-pepper hair and adjusting his tie in a way that comically reminded me of Johnny Carson on the Tonight Show.

Knowing he was very late, he asked me in a whisper if the wedding ceremony was still going on. His liquored breath told me he had jump-started the celebration, so I decided to keep an eye on him as he picked up his seating card and made his way into the garden to catch the final words from the minister.

Within a couple of minutes the musicians struck up Mendelssohn's traditional recessional tune and the officially married couple retreated to a private room to savor the moment before rejoining their guests poolside for cocktails. I checked in on Meg and John to see if they were ready to join their guests and Meg was touching up her make-up and John was pacing, seemingly anxious to join their guests. Meg took a final swig of her wine, finishing the wine filled bolo glass while John's goblet was hardly touched.

Meanwhile, our sauced late guest was making the rounds, glass in hand, enjoying himself thoroughly. I gave the high sign to the bartender to pour very lightly if Charlie wanted any further gin and tonics.

As hosts of their own wedding, John and Meg opened the dinner reception by warmly welcoming their guests. A toast from the best man followed, after which the feasting began. John and Meg, wine glasses in hand, strolled from table to table chatting with their guests oblivious to what was going on just a few yards from them.

I didn't see Charlie seated at his assigned table so I scanned the tent and spotted him visiting tables on the other side of the tent. Anchoring his teetering form by throwing his arms over the shoulders of two guests to steady himself, he slurred out a story his captive audience strained uncomfortably to understand.

When he finally lurched away, the guests just shook their heads and resumed eating. Before Charlie could plant himself at another table, the maid of honor and I signaled each other to head Charlie off at the pass to avoid further embarrassment for everyone. The maid of honor had overheard Charlie telling a raunchy story about a weekend tryst he and Meg had several years ago. In the best interest of the bride and groom I decided the party was over for Charlie.

Fortunately Tom, the owner of the estate, was home for the evening and agreed to help me get the drunken guest out of the way until security patrolling the borders of the property could reach us. I tapped Charlie on the shoulder and told him there was a phone call for him inside the house. As soon as he was inside, I ushered him into the den, far away from the party and locked the doors.

After Tom and I got Charlie to sit down, we told him we didn't think he wanted to hurt Meg by telling inappropriate stories of long ago. He sank deeper into the soft leather couch and began sobbing about painful feelings he had suppressed for years. He explained that after he and Meg broke up, he buried away his true feelings so they could maintain a friendship. The news of the wedding had ripped the wound wide open.

Thankfully, John and Meg never learned the full extent of Charlie's gross behavior the night of the wedding.

After about thirty minutes and two cups of coffee, Charlie agreed that he should leave the party. After two failed attempts to convince him to let us call him a cab, I had no choice but to call the police as he left in the courtesy van to warn the police of a driver who had been drinking would be heading for the canyon route home.

Later in the week I heard through the grapevine that Charlie had come to his senses and realized that driving in the canyon was not a good idea. He stopped at one of the first turn-outs and called a friend to pick him up.

Unlucky in love, Charlie nonetheless drew an ace in having a good friend who got him home safely after an evening of less-than-discreet behavior.

Epilogue:

It is best not to invite old paramours to a wedding. You never know what they will do or say, especially when the liquor is flowing.

Unfortunately for John and Meg, they started living apart shortly after they exchanged vows when she realized she just wasn't cut out for married life and was happier living solo..

In this story the happy ending goes to John who found true love a few years later; today they are married and his wife is pregnant with their first child.

Chapter 9

Ode to the Perfect Princess Bride

If ever, while dressing your Barbie and Ken dolls in wedding attire, you wished upon a star, imagining your someday-walk down the aisle in your big puffy ball gown...well, this story is for you.

Now, find a comfortable spot to rest for a while. Set aside the milk and cookies; you can't get any crumbs on this page. Rebecca wouldn't like it. Rebecca loved pretty things, but her mother had strict rules about how she kept her clothes and when she could wear them. She got used to playing by her mom's rules.

When I met Rebecca and her mom for the first time in my home office, I was impressed on how mannerly and respectful Rebecca seemed. She looked so sophisticated in her six-inch heels and designer bag that held all her wedding notes and inspirational photos.

Tall, curvaceous and bright, Rebecca sat sweetly on my chocolate velour love seat — knees together, feet forward — and gushed forth twenty-plus years of romantic yearnings for the fairytale wedding she envisioned. Rebecca dreamed of walking into the church heralded by a trumpet fanfare as organ music surged from the exposed pipes to the side of the high altar. On her father's arm she would walk the ninety-foot aisle with grace and reverence, drinking in the sight of her handsome groom beaming back at her as she moved ever closer and closer to him.

Then she imagined entering the ballroom and being led to the table on the dais by her new husband and finding it adorned with shimmering candles encased in lace, gilded candelabras and velvety flower petals creating a rippling gold-on-gold river. Even the likes of Louis XIV would have bestowed his pleasure on this setting.

Rebecca was determined that nothing would mar her quest for the picture-perfect wedding. She held to her word when the wedding day arrived. No hiccups dampened her soaring spirits — not late relatives and bridesmaids who delayed the pre-ceremony photo shoot, not the testy church wedding director, the antsy flower girls, not even the last minute substitution of the pedigreed antique white Rolls Royce that had been procured to whisk her from the Church to the private club for dinner, dancing and their first night as husband and wife. Nothing put a dent in her utter enjoyment of this fairytale wedding.

Immediately following the ceremony the guests exited the church and made the ten-mile drive through city traffic to the upscale coastal private club. As the clock struck 8:00 PM the ballroom doors opened to the aaaahs of the invited guests. They were treated to a kaleidoscope of crystal and gold décor set against chiffon-draped walls that framed a gleaming dance floor with the couple's initial monogrammed in gold. The tables glittered with flatware, wine glasses, bread baskets, and salt and pepper shakers all touched with gold accents. The final touch, menus embedded in white and gold edible chocolate encased in cellophane, sat perched atop each place setting.

Just one dance with her husband before dinner was served for our lady Rebecca. This princess bride didn't want to perspire and ruin her make-up before the last formal photos were taken at the cake cutting immediately following the main course.

Once the welcoming words from the parents of the bride were spoken and the best man's toast completed, the guests were treated to a four-course meal. With her Prince Charming by her side, Rebecca strolled from table to table warmly greeting her guests and expressing gratitude for coming to witness the nuptials and share the feast.

No dancing in between courses; these guests gutted it out through 90-plus minutes of serve, consume, and clear.

Immediately following the dessert course, Rebecca retouched her make-up tableside. Gazing into the mirror of a bejeweled compact, she powered her nose, cheeks, and chin and then, after two quick strokes of lipstick, pressed her lips together, sealing her crimson smile.

As Rebecca and her husband made their way to the middle of the dance floor to say their thank-yous and cut the cake, it was time to bring out the last little surprise for the guests. Placed in a storeroom adjoining the ballroom were baskets of pink slippers for the women to swap with their heels when dancing got underway after dinner.

A special pair of white leather slippers for Rebecca had been placed on the top of one of the baskets — but when the baskets were brought out and set on the floor next to the band stage, the white slippers were nowhere to be found.

I alerted the catering staff immediately and, as the cake was being cut and served, we hunted everywhere for the missing bridal slippers, but no luck. After the cake ritual and the father/daughter and mother/son dance, I quietly told Rebecca about the missing slippers. To the staffs' great relief, she nodded and shrugged her shoulders. Then, donning a pair of pink slippers, she danced her heart out to the top 40 tunes of the day.

During a brief band break the guests finished the last of the wedding cake and coffee, some saying their goodbyes and wishing the couple well. Those who remained returned to the white shiny floor for the final dance set. Just before midnight Rebecca checked her make-up one more time before the last dance and the final photo opp.

The photographer darted about the room capturing the last embraces on the dance floor and the tossing of the bouquet. Rebecca and her husband waved goodnight to their guests from the landing of the staircase just around the corner from the ballroom. Finally, they ascended the staircase to their awaiting honeymoon suite. It was a fitting finale and, aside from the missing slippers, a smashingly successful reception.

To Rebecca, it was a storybook wedding day. Less composed brides would have been fraught with frustration and disappointment over the minor glitches and missteps of others. Such trivial concerns didn't deter her from celebrating and enjoying herself to the fullest. She had both the youthful optimism and the mature wisdom to appreciate everything her wedding team did to perfect her cherished day. She got what she wanted most: The beautiful church ceremony, the gorgeous wedding reception, the décor she dreamed of, and her Prince Charming. What more could she ask for!

The answer: A mother willing to do a lot of grunt work! As Rebecca and her husband disappeared into wedded bliss, the mother of the bride thanked everyone for a job well done and left me with the words, "Let's talk soon."

Rebecca's mom became the Monday morning coach conducting a recap session over the phone with her quarterback coordinator — me. The hour-long post mortem featured a frustrated mother-of-the-bride recounting each misstep and how-come beginning with, "How dare the groom's family be so inconsiderate to show up late for photos delaying the groomsmen who were supposed to be helping seat the guests."

Even after a formal music rehearsal in which each piece was meticulously mapped and cued, requiring overtime pay for the musicians, the trumpets came in two bars early while the soloist was a little sharp on the last note of her second song. Even the up-lights the church director said we could have on both sides of the sanctuary fell short of expectations after needing to be placed much farther apart than first promised, definitely diminishing the intended effect.

She continued. The special gate brought in by the floral designer was a less-than-perfect fit for the doorway leading into the sanctuary that framed the wedding party processional.

And then the Rolls Royce…

Did I forget to mention that the wooden 'Rolls Royce' plaque that had been inlaid on the back of the front seats that marked this vehicle as the very one once owned by the fourth Earl of Hampshire…was missing, making this vehicle a sham, an impostor and a pretender to the hand-picked motor carriage that was selected to transport this royal looking couple on their wedding day. Rebecca's mother wanted to know how such a bait and switch maneuver occurred.

I felt so badly for the length Rebecca went to obtain this specific vehicle, I promised to get to the bottom of this issue for Rebecca and her mother. After three telephone calls going up the chain of command to the office of the president of the motor company, the truth came out that the original historic vehicle had been sold a day or two before the wedding. The model that had idled in front of me on the wedding day was its lessor next of kin. Deep breathing time for sure just knowing how much effort Rebecca had put into locating the proper historic vehicle.

To minimize the bride's probable disappointment, I had asked the florist to place a piece of silk over the back of the front seat to conceal the missing inlay and drape it with flowers for added romance. To no avail; after entering the vehicle, Rebecca was so excited and removed the fabric to show the inlay to her now husband…and the jig was up.

The kicker came when the driver asked for payment directly from the bride and groom when they arrived at the club immediately following their church post ceremony photos. I wished the driver had waited to ask me about payment at the club's curbside. When the bride and groom couldn't produce a viable credit card between them, I offered my card and the couple emerged from the Rolls with smiles for the photographer.

The M.O.B. understood the situation and reimbursed me immediately as soon as I informed her of the incident during our Monday morning recap.

The rest of the hits, misses and near misses were dissected and analyzed with surgical precision. This mother-of-the-bride wanted perfection for her loving daughter not only out of love, but because her daughter had contributed to the wedding budget herself from her savings to produce this fantasy wedding. I should have taken my fairy godmother's wand in for a tune-up before this wedding day for sure.

The mystery of how those white leather slippers went missing will always haunt me. I put them in the basket, set them aside literally ten feet from the main reception room in a storeroom, and — poof — they were gone.

This well meaning, conscientious mother had done everything in her power to give her daughter a perfect wedding and the fairytale couple lived happy ever after — for two years!

I'm afraid that — in reality — not everything gilded is golden.

Chapter 10

My Crazy Cake Story

My bride, Andrea, was searching for a creative wedding cake when by coincidence she spotted a beautiful cake in a jewelry store window. She was so impressed with the design and shape of the cake; it was ingeniously designed to look like a wedding ball gown instead of a standard three-tiered wedding cake.

The fondant icing covering the large bottom layer resembled the soft folds of the gown skirt, similar to what Andrea was planning to wear on her wedding day. The middle layer was a take-off on a beaded bodice made from tiny edible crystal beads. On the top layer of the cake little white flowers made of gum paste were arranged to form a confectionery flower nosegay.

Andrea took a snapshot of the jewelry store window cake and sent it to her fiancé, Ronald, to get his opinion. Andrea and Ronald were making all the important decisions together and Ronald was particularly looking forward to picking out and tasting the cake. Since the cake cost was a part of the catering agreement with the hotel, Andrea was confident that even if the hotel had to charge a little extra for the unusual design, their budget could handle it.

Andrea sent me the image and asked me to consult with the hotel pastry chef about reproducing the cake for her wedding. I asked if she had any idea of the dimensions of the cake in the window and she estimated that all three layers measured from 14 to 16 inches high. From eyeballing the image, I figured that the cake would probably serve about 75 to 100 guests, the top layer being made of nonedible, decorative gum-paste flowers. Andrea and Ronald were planning to have at least 350 guests. I told Andrea I would check to see who might have designed the cake and ask them for permission to use their cake design for my client's wedding.

She was surprised that I would need permission to use the design, but I explained that some designers consider their cake designs to be signature pieces that represent their company's style. They discourage copycats. For all I knew, the cake in the window might have been commissioned by the jewelry store, in which case the store might own the rights to that specific design.

The cake's particular style and details suggested to me that it was the creation of a certain well-known cake designer whose work is often showcased in wedding magazines and on TV. I offered to do some investigation and, sure enough, my gut instinct was correct. The cake designer and I had worked together infrequently over many years, but enough for me to recognize her style. The ideas and presentation of the cake in the photo were so special, I just had a feeling it was Margaret's work.

But having found the designer did not assure that the design would work for Andrea and Ronald's wedding. The plain truth is, not every cake design can be enlarged or downsized as easily as one might think. Margaret listened to my concerns about needing a much larger cake and I asked her if that was possible to scale the design up to 350 guest servings.

Margaret said she created the original design specifically to be displayed in the jewelry store window and, frankly, she saw only problems trying to scale up the cake size.

She explained that rolling out fondant in one piece to cover a 12-inch bottom layer is very doable, but having to make the bottom layer at least 24 inches high would be really tough, given the weight of the single sheet of fondant that would have to measure 58 inches in diameter to cover the sides and top of the biggest layer.

Margaret suggested doing a faux cake with real cake on a corner of the bottom layer that could be sliced into for the cake cutting ceremony. She also proposed using back sheet cakes with buttercream icing to ease labor and material costs, and then returning the faux cake to the baker at the end of the evening to be used as a studio model if so desired.

My major concern was cost: Would the per-person price plus the long distance delivery fee and set-up charges exceed the hotel's contracted fee of $10(2005 prices) per person? I was hopeful that the hotel might allow an outside cake company to make this cake design since it was a bit tricky to produce.

Here's what went down.

After my phone conversation with Margaret, I understood the challenges involved in scaling up the wedding cake, but at the same time I wanted to bring my bride's vision to fruition.

The work involved in creating the internal columns needed to support such a large bottom tier plus all the other tiers, along with the necessary technical detail would be both extensive and expensive. Margaret's best price was $18 per person including delivery and set up charges.

When I conveyed the cost to Andrea and Ronald they were silent for a moment. They had been expecting that the cost of the cake might exceed their original budget, but to have the price nearly double was more than they could justify spending.

I told them I totally understood and I asked if it would be okay if I spoke to the hotel and Margaret again to see if she would let someone else bake and design a similar cake with her receiving a design fee for her original design. Andrea, who was beginning to doubt that she would ever have the cake of her dreams, said, "Go for it, Tobey and let's see what the bottom line is going to be."

Once the hotel's pastry chef got a good look at the cake design, it was clear that he was in no hurry to bake this cake. He was amenable to letting someone else do it as long as he would have a way to recoup some of the profit lost from the catering contract. So the hotel suggested they would charge Andrea and Ronald four dollars for the cake cutting fee and call it a day. That was understandable, but now the cake was costing twenty-two dollars a slice, totally over the top for their budget.

Having put hours and hours into solving this cake puzzle, I was hell bent on finding a way to make it work for everyone. But how? I had to find a way to get the price closer to fourteen dollars per slice, the top of the original budget for the client. If I could convince Margaret to let the hotel or another bakery she respected make the cake, perhaps she would be satisfied with a design fee paid to her by the client. Sure enough, the second piece of the cake puzzle was solved when the designer accepted four hundred dollars for the design concept.

In the end, I had approximately thirteen dollars per person to use to produce this cake. The job now was to find a bakery closer to the wedding reception site willing to take on this project for only twelve dollars per person. The cake gods were with me; I found an excellent bakery that was willing to do the job as long as they could do their own interpretation of the design, plus they would keep the faux cake as a studio sample so they might be able to make the cake again for a better profit. Out of respect for the original cake designer, they agreed not to copy the cake exactly; frankly, they too, thought it would be nearly impossible to scale up the original design.

After a long talk with the second bakery we got the price to a total of fourteen dollars per person, which included the four dollars cutting fee for the hotel, the four hundred dollar design fee for the original cake designer, and approximately ten dollars per person for the second bakery to bake the cake, deliver it, and do the set up. The second bakery would supply a drawing of the revised cake to be approved by the bride and groom before moving forward. Everyone involved agreed to the terms and conditions.

Each of us sacrificed some profit to be a part of this project, including me. I didn't charge the bride and groom for the extra time it took to investigate and negotiate the deal, which was above the service level we had originally agreed to.

The clients were very happy with the outcome. For me, it was worth going the extra mile to fulfill a bride and groom's wish for their dream wedding cake. The bonus for everyone came when the wedding was selected to be featured on a well-known wedding reality TV show.

Chapter 11

The Perils of Protocol

Being a wedding planner, I find myself directing traffic at the intersection of past traditions and modern sensibilities. Weddings are steeped in rituals and protocols that must be tempered with modern norms as couples and their guests strive for the perfect balance of meaningful traditions and contemporary social standards.

As I navigate these waters on behalf of my clients, I inevitably revisit my own upbringing and recall wistfully how people honored the protocol of social dressing. As a young person, I looked forward to certain formalities. I liked the feeling of getting dressed up and feeling that something special was about to happen.

Being a child in the mid 1950's and 1960's, I can still remember men wearing hats, jackets, and ties every workday. There were no casual Fridays. Shopping and dining excursions were also more formal. I can still picture my mom behind the steering wheel with gloved hands taking my younger sister and me to the tearoom in Bullocks department store. We politely ate our favorite dessert of ice cream log cake drizzled with chocolate syrup while elegant women modeling the latest fashions strolled through the dining room, stopping and offering details about the outfits they were wearing.

Even a quick trip to the bank was regarded as a business appointment, requiring "appropriate attire" that included a hat and gloves to respect the protocol of a financial institution.

If you were affluent enough to belong to a country club or even a private swim club, age-old rules of conduct and attire were stringently enforced for everyone's well-being, it was thought.

Today, private country clubs and a few exclusive restaurants are the last bastions of such exacting wardrobe standards. Most country clubs that host weddings for non-members still enforce their own branding protocols when it comes to dress and behavior. Some may think it archaic, old fashioned and unrealistic to ask people to abide by these rules, given more casual, contemporary standards that exist today.

By contrast, modern weddings can be extremely eclectic in style as guest attire is often left to the guests' interpretation of phrases like these in today's wedding invitations: "Fabulously dressed women and men duded out." The one rule still honored among upper-crust private clubs today is: No denim or anything mimicking denim is allowed, whether the material is blue, black, pink, or any other color of the rainbow.

Having grown up in – and accepted – an era of occasion-appropriate dress, plus being a business woman who believes in traditional attire, I hardly expected to be the one nabbed for violating the dress code on the day I met a client and her mother at a country club wearing a beige cotton waist-length jacket.

Upon a closer look, the reception desk manager asked me to accompany her to an adjoining room where she personally pointed out that my jacket had grommets and small metal studs with denim-style stitching. She told me I must remove the beige cotton jacket if I wanted to attend the meeting with my client.

I was totally embarrassed to be called out for such a minor infraction. I felt like a misfit, out of place, and for a second, not worthy of being in this exclusive golf and tennis haven. I dutifully removed the jacket, which the receptionist held for me in her office. I then spent two hours freezing under an air conditioning vent in the last vacant chair in the catering director's office.

Some time ago while coordinating a wedding at this same club, the catering manager had put me in a bad spot when he politely told me to ditch my professional two-way radio, the use of which was not mentioned in their rules. I resorted to sneaking around in bathrooms and elevators like a clandestine operative, using my radio only when absolutely necessary since cell phones were banned as well. I have to admit I got a good workout that day running up and down stairs and around corners to the point of getting dizzy to make sure everything was going as planned.

Many of my wedding couples, along with their friends, don't relate to the dress requirements of these very tony clubs, but they choose them nonetheless for their beautiful settings. So I make it my business to warn my clients that dress and conduct codes are still strictly enforced.

It's not surprising that one of my wedding couples, Mark and Susie, were scratching their heads trying to decide what wording to use on their fall wedding invitations at a well-respected country club with a world-class golf course. They just fell in love with the Georgian architecture and graciousness of the surrounding landscape and event spaces. The club found a sponsor for them since they were not members. Mark was a busy businessman and Susie had finished medical school and was waiting to find out in what city and hospital she would be doing her residency.

Personally, they had no problem with the club's rules and regulations, but they knew most of their friends were casual dressers; for the men getting dressed up meant wearing a pair of clean jeans with a white, long-sleeved button-down shirt. The last time these friends dressed up formally was — NEVER. The couple didn't want to put their friends to the expense of renting tuxes and formal attire.

An unpretentious pair, Mark and Susie didn't feel the need to have all the wedding guests dressed as formally as they were going to be, but at the same time they were bound by the club's rules. The only absolute no-no at the club was denim. They decided that if ties and jackets were requested on the invitation, surely the guests would understand the implied need for a pair of slacks and some kind of tie and jacket, right? Actually, I tried to get them to request suits and ties for men and dressy attire for the ladies, meaning cocktail dresses rather than long gowns. If the evening turned out to be a temperate one, as expected, the men could definitely remove their jackets on the dance floor while working up a sweat, which was often the case after dinner.

Southern California delivered a lovely October evening for Mark and Susie's wedding. Gentle breezes and warm temperatures made it possible for the ladies to shed their wraps early for the al fresco ceremony and outside cocktail hour before going inside for dinner and dancing.

There was quite an array of outfits on view as the guests began arriving shortly before the ceremony call time of four o'clock. Ladies displaying varying degrees of plunging necklines, super high six-inch heels, and clingy fabrics dotted the landscape alongside men clad in sport coats and slacks, some with ties, others with just shirts and ties, sans jackets. It wasn't until the beginning of the cocktail hour when the catering captain and I spotted a wardrobe violator, a guest wearing a pair of jeans with a jacket and tie.

The captain and I went over to the gentleman and politely interrupted the guest's conversation with friends, took him aside and gently told him of the strict policy of the club. He said he had one pair of slacks at home but they were ripped and he didn't have time to get another pair. We offered to accompany him to the pro shop on property to buy a pair of pants and he consented. In fact, he was even willing to pay up to $200 for the slacks, but none fit him due to his very generous waistline. The general manager was contacted to see if we could bend the rules, but the request was declined.

Fortunately, the guest was good humored about a situation that could have become very tense. He agreed to leave the club and see if he could find something to wear. He did comment that he read the invitation and it said guests should wear ties, but it didn't forbid wearing jeans. We empathized with him but had to conform to the rules of the house. This was one time when "tying one on" just didn't do the trick.

Lesson learned: Sometimes it's best to listen to the voice of experience and not march to your own drummer. It's best to pass along a friendly blueprint for the highest level of attire the host will be comfortable having their guests wear. Luckily, this time it was just one person, but unfortunately for the guest, he didn't return and missed a lively reception.

Chapter 12

Biting off More than you can Chew can be More than a Hard Swallow

We have all been there once or twice, and if we are really honest, probably several times. We convince ourselves that we have the time, energy and experience to accomplish more than we are used to doing. We take the leap of faith, believing that if the will is there, a way will be found to make it happen.

When this happens in the wedding industry, the client and service alike are opening themselves up to added stress, anxiety and unanticipated expense as they scramble to right the situation – not to mention exposing the client to possible disappointment.

My client, Carol, was very impressed with the flowers she saw at a friend's wedding. She fell in love with the style and colors, and felt confident that this same florist could do a wonderful job for her wedding several months away. The best part was the price. After comparing two other florists' proposals, the total cost of the flowers from her friend's florist was just too good to pass up, so Carol brought on Stella as the florist.

Carol printed out literally dozens of images from Pinterest and other online webpages depicting a dramatic ceremony with swags of white sheer fabric draping the oversized metal and stone columned gazebo. She told Stella what she wanted in the way of other blossoms for the gazebo area, a petal-designed aisle, and backs of chairs on either side of the aisle.

Since I had an abbreviated service plan with Carol, I was only invited to the final floral meeting with the client and her parents. That's when I realized that the florist had never attempted fabric swaging before. But she said she would only charge Carol $100 to place the fabric if Carol would supply the fabric.

I honestly became immediately worried when I heard $100 for what I could perceive would take at least a crew of three a couple of hours of installation and then about another thirty minutes of removal.

Carol agreed to the money, but her face fell when after learning that even though Stella had previous experience doing flower décor on gazebos, she had no idea how to estimate the yardage needed for draping.

I couldn't help thinking that the florist may have overestimated her resources and skills to take this event on. The chance to work at a beautiful property with a chance to wow her clients and the site might have urged Stella beyond her capabilities and knowledge in some areas of design.

I stepped in and suggested my client contact the company supplying the linens for the wedding. Perhaps they kept sheer fabric on hand to sew overlays and could supply it at cost, saving everyone a lot of trouble, time and money. Since the florist's studio was a good two hours from the wedding site, I offered to go back to the site to measure the gazebo and estimate the amount of yardage needed. It was clear to me that I needed to pinch-hit here so we could take this issue off the table as soon as possible.

Unfortunately, the linen provider didn't have the type of fabric the bride needed. I ended up calling another florist who lived pretty close to the fabric warehouses in town and he graciously picked up a 50-yard bolt and dropped it off at my home office a few days later when he was in my neck of the woods. I ordered plenty of fabric just in case the florist ran into trouble and didn't follow the golden rule of installation: measure twice, cut once.

I took a deep breath and said a prayer for the wedding day, now just two weeks away. But I just couldn't shake the "what ifs". What if the florist didn't have enough crew for this installation? What if the florist didn't leave enough time for installation and tear down? What if she didn't have the necessary tools? I decided to call Stella to put my mind to rest.

After several attempts to reach her, we finally talked over the phone five days out from the wedding. I reminded her of the dimensions of the gazebo. I asked her if she had a ten-foot ladder and how many crew she had to do the fabric draping.

Her answer? "I don't have a ten-foot ladder, but I will bring my husband and another assistant to help me." Now I got worried for real. No tall ladder? Unless she could shimmy up the columns and swing like a monkey from the filigree ironwork above, we were in deep you know what!

I called the location to ask if they would let us borrow their ladder, but liability issues nixed that option. I knew the job would take two or three people working up to three hours to complete the swaging, which Stella's timetable didn't allow for.

Still unknown to me was Stella's plan for how long the swaging would take on the wedding day or who would be responsible for taking the material down.

I finally asked Stella if she would be okay with me finding another company to install the fabric, as long as the clients agreed to it. I heard a big sigh over the phone and Stella said that would be terrific. I don't know what Stella was thinking when she then said she would "try and help them" by draping the fabric. Even though it was really generous of Stella to try and help in some way when her client's wishes outgrew the original scope of the job, lets face it, "trying" just doesn't cut it on the wedding day.

Stella needed to find a way to make it right - bottom line - even if that meant bringing in another expert to get it done. An enterprising business owner uses these situations to their advantage by assisting the expert while learning the ins and outs of the task, even if it means taking a loss on the job. Stella's newfound skills would have paid off next time a request came in to work with fabric.

It fell to me to explain this situation to the client since it was my idea to bring someone else in and inform them of the additional costs that would be incurred by bringing in a décor/rental company, assuming I could find one who could squeeze in another job in the five days left before the wedding.

I did find a company and they agreed to do the job on their way to another job in the same area, but the installation would need to start by seven in the morning at the latest. Now, I should have been thrilled with this news, but I knew that someone would need to oversee the job since Carol had very specific desires about the fabric hanging that can't always be communicated in a photo or even with careful note taking.

Finally, someone needed to be available to take down the swaging at the end of the evening, someone who had watched as the draping was installed and was able to deconstruct it without too much trouble.

You guessed it: That person ended up being me. The florist wasn't going to stay and the installing company was going to be deconstructing another event so I anointed myself "Tsarina of Fabric Tear Down," my duties commencing at precisely twelve-thirty in the morning.

My time commitment for the wedding day had just jumped from twelve-plus hours to seventeen-plus hours. I'm not a clock-watcher, but five extra hours of supervision was too much to absorb without some additional compensation, plus the time for all the arranging to make this proper draping possible.

Instead of charging my client for the hours directly, I decided to address the real issue: My personal logistics for the day and how I was to be at my best for the entire stretch of the event. Hot, muggy weather was predicted and the location was too far away to permit me to drive back and forth twice on the wedding day morning to help with the installation, shower and change and be ready to go by noon to begin my other official duties for the wedding.

I asked the bride and groom if they would be willing to pay for a basic hotel room at the same site where the wedding was to be held. I would conduct the rehearsal on Friday night and just stay over so I could roll out of bed early the next morning and take care of the installation and then get back to the room, shower and change for the rest of the day.

This solution would cost Carol less than a third of what they would have paid if I billed them for the extra consulting/research and labor hours. Even though I had solved the problem with the installation, Carol's fiancé was solely focused on the added expense, which I totally understood. Any contingency funds they had budgeted in had been all ready been spent on other extras. In an effort to mitigate the extra expense, Carol asked if the father of the groom could oversee the installation since he was very handy and wouldn't mind.

While I was somewhat relieved by the offer, I had to explain that the father of the groom would need to be able to tell me exactly how the fabric was installed so I could deconstruct it at the end of the evening. Carol took a day to consider my offer and decided (wisely) to pay for my room and let me supervise the gazebo installation and deconstruct it at the end of the evening.

I reminded the groom that my greatest desire was to have the entire family and wedding party completely immersed in the joy of the wedding day, unburdened by the responsibility of making an important element of the wedding day work.

When someone tells you they are not proficient at something, it's best to adjust your expectations accordingly. When a service says they want to help you out by "trying" to perform a task, that's your cue to not be disappointed if it doesn't work out the way you envisioned and be prepared to not see the finished product.

The florist had the best intentions and did a lovely job with the reception dinner centerpieces. The prices were beyond reasonable and, in fact, when I saw the invoice, I remarked to the client that she got the deal of the century. But a deal made and agreed to is a deal that must be done to the specifications and expectations of the client. If not, everyone is disappointed. In this case, the florist felt she over delivered on the flowers and made everything look great, but that didn't make up for the extra cost in labor and time to get the gazebo looking the way the client had envisioned and thought she had paid for.

I share this story with you not to embarrass the hopeful florist, but rather to explain how good intentions, without proper preparation, can lead to a potential disaster. In the end, I convinced Stella to pay for half of the cost of the labor on the gazebo as a sign of good faith for her client, Carol, and to avoid a dissatisfied review on a popular wedding website.

Conclusion

Why it is so Hard to Say so Long

I was looking up a calligrapher's contact information online the other day so I could pass it along to a client. As the page loaded, an orchestral version of "The Way You Look Tonight" surged through my computer speakers as the artful calligraphy rolled across the page. If ever a melody evoked romance…

I began tearing up, so vividly did the music revive memories of countless first dances I have watched over the years. Some of the couples were so natural in their movements, gliding across the dance floor, effortlessly performing their steps. Other couples, the less-skilled dancers, intently counted the beats, monitoring their every step, nodding reassurances to each other, making me wonder if they were enjoying this moment at all.

Every time a couple walks on the dance floor I get that anxious feeling in my stomach like I'm watching my children ride their bikes without training wheels for the first time. Just as my kids made it happen for themselves —flawed or perfectly executed — my couples always got through the final sway, turn, and dip.

With every step they perform, I am right there in my imagination hoping that their first steps as husband and wife go well; perhaps I'm looking for an omen of a good marriage to come.

Lets face it. I'm an incurable romantic. If there is such a thing as a romance gene in your DNA, I've got it in spades. I believe this attachment to romance has kept me in this business for 25 years. I have developed a certain Zen patience that allows me to handle the avalanche of client emotions while still balancing a slew of wedding services to assure conditions are favorable for them to deliver the goods, making our client happy at the end of the day. The satisfaction I get from a job well done ultimately rewards my faith in romance.

How, then, am I going to step away from this profession of romance? I, who am helplessly hooked whenever I encounter the promise of love. The thought of stepping back from the job of wedding planner and no longer witnessing those intimate, tender and joyous moments is tough to imagine. Yet, as my clients go on to face the ups and downs of married life, I know that the six-hour event I helped plan and execute will recede into a faint blip on the radar of their life together.

Still, it is huge to me.

Some years ago I watched a film that really touched me. It was called "Dad" and featured Ted Danson as the son and Jack Lemmon as the father. The dying father was quite a character. He made his wife, played by Olympia Dukakis, really suffer at times, and yet they had many moments of great exhilaration and joy over the 40-plus years of their marriage.

At one point, Lemmon's character strikes a pose in a doorway of their modest house wearing a Hawaiian shirt that reminded me of how my father used to joke around. Just like Lemmon in the film, my dad, in his colorful Hawaiian shirt, gazed upward, one hand on a hip, the other arm reaching up and touching the opposite corner of the door jam, striking the pose of an ancient Roman statue, silly expressions on their faces. It always made me laugh.

The scene finishes with Danson and Dukakis having a drink at the kitchen table. Dukakis admits that life with his father hasn't been a piece of cake. But despite all the ups and downs, if she could do it all over again, she wouldn't have married anyone else.

You get the feeling watching this scene that maybe Ted's mother is really telling her son not to give up on his own foundering marriage.

She goes on to describe her marriage to his father as the difference between a merry-go-round and a roller coaster. She could have chosen someone who would have given her a safe, secure, and predictable life. But when she met his dad, she knew he was a firecracker; there would be plenty of sparks between them as they traveled an uncertain path filled with adventure and possibilities. She chose the roller coaster ride with few regrets.

I feel the same way about my decision to start my wedding business. I knew there were safer and more predictable options out there, but I couldn't resist the romantic adventure into a business based on the promise of love.

When I was contemplating starting my wedding business, my dad had already passed away, depriving me of his good council. My mother urged me to go back to teaching, even if it meant moving out of the area that we made home for more than ten years. She wanted me to be safe and to know what the future held.

It wasn't until I took the leap and experienced what it was like to help couples get down the aisle that I knew I had found my calling. All the long days and nights, the endless phone calls, countless meetings, and continuous email exchanges. The occasional disappointments offset by passion and touching tales of love — all this and more fed my soul and gave me purpose.

Even today, when a new couple walks into my office, I gaze at them sitting side-by-side on the loveseat and wonder about the possibility of their happiness together. As I watch how they look at each other, how they touch — or not touch — each other, how close they sit, I try to imagine them ten, twenty years in the future and wonder if they will be as happy then as they seem today. I don't have a crystal ball and I haven't kept records, but I do sense the difference between a couple that is relaxed and in sync and a couple that is anxious and uneasy making decisions together.

I made the difficult decision earlier this year that 2014 would be my last year as a full-time event and wedding planner. My once bustling business has been contracting slowly over the last four years due to some physical challenges that I could no longer ignore.

I came to an impasse. I had to face the fact that I wasn't enjoying my business as much as I once did. I began experiencing a shift in my personal priorities and state of mind, followed, sadly, by the passing of my older sister, Merill. Suddenly, I realized life was giving me an unwanted but much-needed wake-up call.

Merill's death made me face the fact that time was rushing by; I had pushed aside my dream of creating artwork for more than two decades. I didn't want to miss the chance to be a productive artist once again.

I remain happily connected to the special event industry, mentoring aspiring wedding planners, advising wedding businesses as to their business goals, and assisting brides and grooms with my online tools to match them up with compatible wedding planners and/or coordinators.

The road ahead may be a bit uncertain, but I have finally learned the value of following your passion and with diligence and commitment I look forward to exploring new possibilities.

Romantic, don't you think?

Author Biography

Tobey Dodge understands the wedding industry from inside out, like few others. She has helped nearly eight hundred families plan their weddings over the last twenty-seven years. She has guided brides and grooms through emotional tug-of-wars, trying to find balance between their expectations and their pocketbooks while striving to create the wedding of their dreams.

Tobey shares stories about her life before becoming a wedding planner that sets the stage for her understanding of families and their cultural and ethnic diversity—from her professional teaching experience and foreign travels as a home-wares designer to her work in nonprofit endeavors for her community center.

She applied her understanding and knowledge of other cultures as she assists her clients' road to the altar. Her skill and aptitude for artfully solving wedding challenges and describing the circumstances facing many families in today's world demonstrates her breath of knowledge and experience, creating the perfect foundation to instruct others through her stories on how to set priorities and handle the unexpected. Tobey ultimately provides the reader with a benchmark to gauge their own expectations, ward off problems before they present themselves, and realize even though a wedding is a reflection of one's passion, self-expression, and dreams, it is also a team effort.

Tobey has been a special event industry leader in Southern California for over two decades. Her professional affiliations include past codirector for the Association of Bridal Consultants, past board member and educational chairperson for the Greater Los Angeles chapter of the International Special Event Society, and past board member and former wish granter for OC/LA chapter of Wish Upon a Wedding, and she has trained and/or mentored over fifty aspiring wedding planners. She also holds the coveted designation of a CSEP (certified special event professional). Her weddings have appeared in many popular publications such as Inside Weddings, People, Celebrations, and US magazine. Her weddings have been documented on TV shows like "Wedding Stories" and "Platinum Weddings."

To follow Tobey:
http://twitter.com/bestwc
www.tobeydodge.com
or www.connect.wedding

Printed in the United States
By Bookmasters